Listen with the ears of your heart!

Feli Sebastian
9/1/20

Broken & Beloved
A Journey of Discovery

By Felicitas "Feli" S. Sebastian, Ph.D.
Edited by Charlene Homan
Touchstone Storytelling LLC

Copyright © 2020 Feli Sebastian
Touchstone Storytelling LLC Bloomington, IL
All rights reserved.

This book is published by
Touchstone Storytelling LLC
Copyright © 2020

All rights reserved.

No portion of this book may be reproduced in any form whatsoever without permission from the author and publisher.

Published in the United States by
Touchstone Storytelling LLC and Feli Sebastian.

TouchstoneStorytelling.com

Names: Felicitas "Feli" S. Sebastian, Ph.D., author
Charlene Homan, editor/publisher/page design

Cover Design and Illustration by Paul McNamara
makegoodcreative.com

DEDICATION

For my parents Miguel and Felisa, my siblings, my husband Jim Moeller, my great friend Mary Campbell, and to all women prisoners and most especially to the women of Labyrinth, who I have learned to love.

Feli, left, and her parents, Felisa and Miguel.

CONTENTS

	Appreciations	i
	Foreword	7
1	PART ONE: *The Making of Me* Early Days In The Philippines: 1946-1962	9
2	Back To University, Leaving Home	17
3	Returning Home; U.S. Calls	20
4	Branching Out	44
5	Reawakening	49
6	Healing	60
7	PART TWO: *The Birth Of Labyrinth* Inspiration	62
8	Labyrinth Is Born	63
9	Labyrinth Shifts Its Focus	70
10	Seek, And You Shall Find	75
11	Evolution	83
12	What's On The Horizon?	96
13	Without Volunteers, Collaborators & Donors, There Would Be No Labyrinth	99
	Extras & Resources	114

My mom and Adey, Fall 2005.

APPRECIATIONS

Many thanks, too, for those who helped support the production of this book. To each of them, my heartfelt gratitude:

Charlene Homan, my editor, for her invaluable expertise and guidance, friendship, empathy, challenge, and laughter. She was ever so patient in helping me recognize there is value in telling my story. She was convinced I have a story to tell that is worth sharing and inspiring.

Paul McNamara, my graphic designer, for the attractive cover of my book. He intuitively knew the message I wanted to express in my story through art.

Ashley Sang, my proofreader, who diligently examined my manuscript and saw to it that everything is in place.

The Monks of St. Bede Abbey in Peru, IL, for providing me a quiet place to write and get re-charged. The Monks have been my "second" family and the Abbey my "second" home for many years.

The Sisters of St. Mary Monastery, Rock Island, IL, for their encouragement and prayers. Their vowed life has guided me to live the Benedictine spirituality.

Miguel and Felisa, my parents, for their unconditional love, their perseverance, and their strong faith in God. These qualities molded my character early in life.

My nine siblings, for their support, respect, and love without which I would have not persevered in every challenge I met in life.

Jim, my husband, for his understanding, patience, and light heartedness. These attributes lessened the load of writing my book. He was always supportive when I needed to get away.

And most of all, to God, for His steadfast presence in my life. I am grateful for all the blessings he has poured into my life and my family's lives.

FOREWORD

My name is Feli Sebastian and I'm writing this memoir to inspire readers to support one another, love one another and to make a difference in the lives of someone else. This is my personal memoir as well as my journey in creating Labyrinth Outreach Services for formerly incarcerated women in McLean County, Illinois. The two stories are interwoven, and as one grew so did the other. For you, dear reader, I have shared both.

I feel blessed to have nurtured this fledgling organization and I know that through the YWCA McLean County's leadership, this non-profit will continue to prosper.

Some people have asked, "Why name the organization Labyrinth? It's hard to spell and may be confusing."

Simply put, a labyrinth is an ancient symbol of life's journey. It symbolizes the many paths our life's journey can take as we walk toward a better tomorrow. The term labyrinth was chosen because it is symbolic of our clients' journeys: the twists and turns of their lives, their defeats, and their triumphs.

The labyrinth dates to the early history of civilization where it was used for many purposes: for healing, for meditation, for answers to people's concerns. Looking deeper, all these purposes have one thread: to help one get to know his/her true self. There are many labyrinths in different parts of the world. The most famous is in the Cathedral of Chartres in Chartres, France. This labyrinth is a little over 42 feet in diameter and is believed to be constructed in the first decades of the 13th century. It is composed of four segments converging in the center. It has been said that walking the labyrinth creates a "miracle" or transformation in the person doing so. Something unseen but internal happens within the person. The experience is deeply personal. I hope to bring others on this road to peace and happiness through their journey with Labyrinth.

In the same way that walking the labyrinth helps us get in touch with who we are, we hope that our Labyrinth clients also discover and re-discover their true personhood. As one client said, "My history is not my destiny." In the labyrinth there are many "dead ends," as is true in each of our lives. What we do with the dead ends shapes our next step.

The labyrinth signifies not just the journey of our women, but also the journey of the organization. I will share with you the many ups and downs (oftentimes a series of downs) we faced as we struggled to build Labyrinth. Let these stories touch your heart and encourage you to walk your personal "labyrinth;" for no matter how hard it is, in the center there is rest, peace and freedom. Freedom to be the person you are meant to be. The women's success stories and mine are filled with freedom and transformation because we recognized and acknowledged who we are meant to be: God's Beloved.

PART ONE
The Making of Me

1 EARLY DAYS IN THE PHILIPPINES: 1946-1962

I am one of ten children and the second oldest. When my eldest brother Jovi decided to enter Catholic seminary in the sixth grade, I was first in line to assist my mother Felisa in raising my younger eight siblings. My father Miguel, who we fondly called "Adey" supported our large family working for Shell Oil Company of the Philippines, and later as an independent contractor for Shell.

I was born in Manila in 1946 and my family and I lived with my maternal grandparents for six years before moving to a rented nipa hut, a stilt-type house indigenous to the area, about 30 minutes northeast of Manila in Quezon City. At the time, we were a family of six. I started school as a first grader and my mother would walk me to school, standing across the street for the first few days to reassure

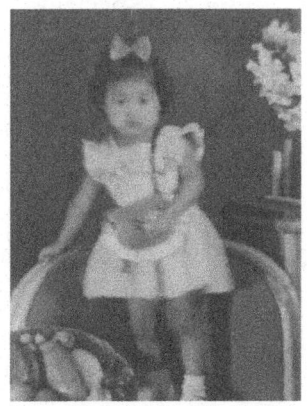

Feli Sebastian, two years old March 5, 1948.

me that she was there. I remember occasionally glancing out the window just to be sure.

She gradually spent less and less time outside the window and soon I was walking to and from school on my own, a short walk of nearly six blocks. During these early years I mastered many things, including cooking rice on the stovetop, which I reached by perching on a short stool. My small hands also smoothed out handkerchiefs and pillowcases with an electric iron, and I laid out clothes to dry on the grassy patch in back where they could be bleached by the sun.

I never felt these chores were burdensome, and I took great care to do them well. When my mother bragged that I had cooked the rice or neatly piled the pillowcases, I swelled with pride. This would be the first of many times my mother would encourage me and urge me to trust in myself.

It was during these formative years that I remember a woman who would visit my mother occasionally. I was awakened by the sound of sobbing and I could make out her slight figure as she was hunched down outside of our mosquito netting. She would reappear from time to time, often with a black eye or fresh bruises. My mother later explained to me that this woman's husband was an abusive alcoholic. I was sad for her, but also happy that she was not my mother. My mom was safe with my Adey. This experience – both this woman's situation and my mother's caring response – helped shape me into the woman I am today, especially when as a young adult I shifted my career from teacher to counselor.

At the tender age of six, I first encountered the miracle of birth. My mother was pregnant with her fifth child. It was near the end of March and school was out for the year. I first heard Ermie's cry while my cousin Lyn and I were checking the hens' coops, hanging on the post under our nipa hut. The two-story structure had an open lower level with a dirt floor. In addition to the coops, it was our playground where we played Jack Stone or Piko, a Filipino version of hopscotch, in the dirt. I was lucky that Lyn lived just next door in a house so big I deemed it a castle.

Upon hearing the baby's cries, I rushed upstairs and waited impatiently until I could enter. I had a new baby brother.

After Ermie was born, my parents began looking in earnest for a larger home. They bought a small narrow lot which was a 25-minute walk from our nipa hut. Located in a new subdivision, the home was one of the first to be built and it was surrounded by long rice fields. With the help of my maternal grandfather and his friends who were skilled carpenters, a two-bedroom, two-story 325-square foot home was built on the site and the Sarmiento-Sebastian clan had a place to call home. On weekends I remember tagging along with my grandfather to watch the house being built. The next five of my siblings were born in the home and we consider it our ancestral home today.

Unbeknownst to us – the five children now living in the U.S. – my brothers – Father Jovi, Toots, and Diko – restored our family home in June 2019. Over a period of several months, the workers disassembled and reassembled every piece of our house: doors, windows, flooring, wooden siding, stairs, roof, iron grills, and the gate. Nearly 95 percent of the original home was restored and now sits on a family compound we've established in Bocaue, Bulacan, some 32 miles

Left, House in the Philippines compound.

Right, The arrows reflect the different places where Feli and her nine siblings resided in as they left their heritage home in Sibuyan, Q.C.

away from the original site. Our Dream House was built on the same lot in 2009, with an outdoor chapel nestled between them.

The restoration was a Christmas gift and a surprise for all of us when we went home for my brother's 50th priesthood celebration in December 2019.

Struggles

My parents always said, "cheaper by the dozen," and like clockwork, my mom would announce a pregnancy every year and a half. I think every generation wants an improvement from their lot in life, and my parents wanted the same for us. My mom was the figurative head of the family, but my dad was the heart. It was always easier to ask Adey for things, because Mom would be a firm, "No, we're on a budget." One of my brothers said it was like being in the military. Looking back, I guess there needed to be order, or else it would have been chaos.

My dad's family struggled, and he didn't finish high school until he was in his 20s because he had to work to support his mother and three siblings. His father had died when he was just five years old. At age 16, he dropped out of school to support his family. He left home and moved to Manila to work in a bowling alley alongside his uncle. Eventually he saved up enough money to return to his studies and finished high school by completing evening courses. Later, in his 60s, he finished a business and accounting degree via correspondence from La Salle Extension College in Michigan.

Miguel Sebastian, my Adey.

My mother had a middle-class upbringing and was one of six siblings, although three were lost in infancy. She completed school and earned a degree in elementary education. Her mother always said, "I'm going to send you to school and you're going to finish. You never know what is going to happen. You need something to fall back on."

Although she didn't return to work as a teacher after she married, she was the primary teacher and caregiver to her ten children. My mother also became an astute businesswoman who sold patis – a dipping sauce made from fermented fish – to neighbors, friends, and locals. Patis is used in many Filipino dishes. She expanded her business and all of us kids worked with her bottling and peddling the patis. At the height of the business, she was probably selling 150-200 bottles a month. Eventually she added other merchandise ranging from Hong Kong-made sweaters and stockings to shoes and vinegar. I also noticed that oftentimes when a tuition bill arrived, my mom would pawn a piece of jewelry she had inherited from her family, who were jewelers by trade. It would usually reappear a few months later when she had worked enough to buy it back.

Justina "Ote" Ma. Sebastian

Even with my father's full-time work and my mother's side business, money was tight. Mom always said, "God will provide," and then she'd be the one to sneak out of the house to peddle more patis. My father was pretty traditional and didn't want her to work, but after he repeatedly witnessed the bags and bags of goods and patis sold, he turned a blind eye to the business. Luckily, my father's sister Ote, who remained single, lived with us and helped take care of us children and the household. She was like a second mom to us.

I entered second grade at a new public school situated within walking distance of our new home. I would walk with my younger brother Diko along the dirt and stone-crushed streets, passing by large homes surrounded by very tall fences. When I entered fifth grade, my commute included a stop to Lourdes Church, just blocks from my school. Sometimes a group of us, but oftentimes just me, would make the trek up two flights of stairs to the Shrine of the Statue of the Blessed Virgin Mary and either kiss or rub her feet, say a quick prayer, and continue on our way.

It was also around this time that I was introduced to a library. I marveled at the shelves and shelves of books. I couldn't believe that I could take any book I wanted! My love affair with reading began around the time I discovered the library. I brought home a book every week and went through each shelf alphabetically. I didn't want to miss a thing! I was studious and reserved by nature and my family didn't have extra money for sports and extracurricular activities, but I was content with my books. My days were filled with reading, caring for my siblings, school, and playing with neighborhood children.

In 1958, I graduated from sixth grade and entered high school. My father enrolled me in MLQ University High School, a private coed school which was farther from home. He had taken classes at this school years before. It was in the heart of Manila, a half-hour commute from home.

My dad showed me the routine of riding a Jeepney, a public bus made from an extended former U.S. military Jeep, which was often crammed with as many people as could fit. We would walk to the stop closest to the house, ride the Jeepney together, and then I would continue my walk to school. Luckily, he took the same Jeepney to his job, so he'd often accompany me in those early days. He oftentimes stopped at the local Catholic church, Church of the Black Nazarene, just blocks from my school. It was a quick stop, maybe three minutes, but I routinely stopped to pray as well. During my four years of high school, I also stopped after school for a quick prayer before heading home. I really give my dad a lot of credit in modeling his devotion to his Catholic faith.

It was around this time that I began to help my mom in her business. I'd sell patis to friends, neighbors, family, and local businesses. My siblings and I would also spend weekends cleaning small glass whiskey bottles donated to us by friends who knew we needed them for bottling the patis. There was a method of washing, sterilizing, and filling the bottles. From high school to the end of my college years, every Sunday after church, my brother Diko and I would go door to door in my grandmother's neighborhood in Manila and sell patis from 10 a.m. to 1 p.m. We walked from street to street with our wicker basket and knocked on doors in the heat, which often reached the upper 90s in the summer. All of us were schooled in the art of the fish sauce business.

My mother trained us all to be proud of our work, no matter how menial it might be. She said do not be embarrassed to knock on a door and sell patis. There is dignity in an honest day's work.

Felisa Sebastian, my mother

I really enjoyed my high school years and met a lot of new friends. I was on the honor roll and was a Society writer and assistant editor of our school paper, in addition to serving as president, secretary, or treasurer in a multitude of school clubs and campus organizations.

I graduated with highest honors from MLQ University High School in 1962 and enrolled in the College of the Holy Spirit, a private college for girls. It was run by the Filipino and German Sisters of the Holy Spirit Missionary Sisters, S.Sp.S. (Latin: Servae Spiritus Sancti). However, I was lonely and felt socially displaced during the first two years at my new school. There were many cliques, but I didn't feel I fit in anywhere. I wanted a close friend, but I was unsure how to seek out someone. That was when Ester Canon-Uson befriended me and changed the course of my remaining years at Holy Spirit. She was pretty and intelligent, but also quiet like me. We quickly became best friends and spent a lot of time together. I became a part of her family and she mine. The remaining years sped by and I graduated from Holy Spirit in 1966 with a bachelor's degree in history, just two semesters shy of earning another degree in education. Upon graduation, Ester got married right away while I searched for the purpose of my life.

My parents always said that although they couldn't leave us an inheritance, they could give us an education. They sacrificed to send us to the best schools. All of us graduated from high school and college, with many of us earning master and doctorate degrees.

Sebastian grads front row, left, sisters Aline, Gelly, Tessie, mom, Felisa, Girlie⁺ and Feli. Back, left, Ray, Toots, Ermie⁺, father, Miguel, Diko, Jovi.

2 BACK TO UNIVERSITY, LEAVING HOME

Growing up in such a large family taught us a lot. Today, all my siblings and I remain close. Our parents always said "Mag-mahalan Kayo," which means to love one another in Tagalog, a language spoken by nearly a quarter of the population in the Philippines. That love and support continues to give me strength.

My family isn't perfect. We fight like crazy. We all have strong convictions. When we have friction, we just take a time out and everyone goes to their corner. But we come back together – always.

> "Our parents always said 'Mag-mahalan Kayo,' which means to love one another in Tagalog."

I finished college in March 1966. As the first child to graduate and get a full-time job, I felt a lot of responsibility to help my family financially. I continued to live at home and went to work for about a year as an extension supervisor for the Student Catholic Action (SCA), where I trained high school students in public schools to become Christian leaders in their communities. That job was short-lived, and later that year I started working as a teacher at Xavier School, a small, private, male school for wealthy Chinese families. I taught basic subjects, including art and music, to boys in preschool/kindergarten and grades one and four. It was around this time when I met Bill, the man who would become the central figure in my life for many, many years.

I was happy with teaching, especially when I worked with each student on individualized reading. It was fun, but also a lot of work. I must have been burnt out after six years because I was soon looking for something else. I took a leave of absence for a year and worked part-time at a Montessori school while I enrolled in a master's program in the evenings at Ateneo de Manila, a Jesuit-run university. I started my degree in history but soon changed to a more marketable degree, administration in education. After a year, I earned a graduate assistant position and then enrolled full-time.

Halfway through my master's degree, the university phased out my program of study. At this point, I chose to study counseling because I felt the work entailed more of a human factor than the other choices on offer. I did my practicum in the grade school associated with the university. Before I finished, one of my professors encouraged me to apply to a program abroad. I was accepted at Indiana University in Bloomington, Indiana but the scholarship was only for part of the fees. I backed out because I lacked the money. Around that time, my dad had retired from Shell and started his own small business selling propane tanks. My mom leased a small sari-sari store, similar to a convenience store in the U.S., to help with our expenses because there were still six children in school. I could not in good conscience ask for money to pursue studying abroad when my siblings were still in school and needed support.

Feli Sebastian, MA graduate, Philippines.

A couple of years later, my mother's industriousness paid off. In 1975, she opened her own sari-sari store. Many neighborhood people shopped at these small stores where they could use credit and purchase staples such as rice, oil, sugar, salt and other perishable goods in smaller quantities. I graduated in 1975 and worked as a guidance counselor at Ateneo de Davao Grade School, another Jesuit-run school in Davao City, Mindanao, the southernmost island in the Philippines. For the first time, I was separated from my family. I was a three-hour plane ride away, and I had mixed feelings about the distance.

At 29-years-old, I was excited to finally experience independence, but I felt guilty leaving my loved ones behind. It was particularly hard leaving my three youngest siblings – Toots, Ray, and Aline – because they were like my own children. The primary reason I accepted the job was because of the salary; 1,000 pesos monthly with benefits and free plane tickets to go home every Christmas and summer vacation which was quite lucrative at the time.

I was the guidance counselor for preschool through grade three while another counselor, Tina Bajo, oversaw grades four to six. I established and organized the school's entrance exam and achievement exams. I found the work easy and I had plenty of time to "play." For the first time, I realized the responsibility of being an adult, being accountable; I relished making decisions on my own. I made a lot of friends who came with me to Manila during the summers. They also became my family's friends.

I was in Davao City for four years. During my final year there, my mom called me to come home as there were a lot of bombings in Davao City. I obliged.

PearlCor, Aguinaldo Pearl Farm, 1978, Samai Island, Davao. From left, Feli, unknown, Zeny Carriedo-Mahipus, unknown. Second row, Gene.

3 RETURNING HOME; U.S. CALLS

I returned home in 1979 and worked in Manila as a principal at the Montessori Co-op School. However, I felt displaced. All the freedoms I had known were gone and I was pushed into my role of daughter, sister, caretaker once again. I wanted to get my own apartment, but my dad was adamantly against it. To keep the peace, I obeyed and resolved to try again in a year's time. Although the pay was good, I didn't enjoy my job. It entailed a lot of administrative work and very little counseling. I stayed for a year, and was even offered a bonus to stay, but I needed to move on. I resigned without a clear future.

By then it was 1980 and my younger sister Tessie had moved to the United States to find her future. My mother accompanied her to Ohio, and I stayed behind to manage Mom's sari-sari store. I managed it for nearly a year and worked to clear all customer debts, added more merchandise to the shelves, and increased the number of customers paying cash. Ten months into the year, my mother returned home. Back in the U.S., Tessie was lonely without family at her side and wanted to return to the Philippines.

Feli Sebastian Ohio, Summer 1981.

It was decided I would visit since I was at loose ends anyway. As the eldest sister, I felt it was my responsibility to support and reassure my parents and siblings.

So, I wound up in Ohio. I had no idea at the time that this would soon become my new home. A change in direction, that's what I thought of, as I stepped off the plane at Chicago's O'Hare airport. I was 35 years old. My Uncle Sixto, my mother's only living brother, picked me up and I strode over to greet him. He had been living in the U.S. since 1972 and it had been nearly 10 years since I had laid eyes on him. We were quick to share a hug and the shift began that would change the trajectory of my life, a life I left behind in the Philippines.

After a week of visiting my uncle and touring Chicago, I made the nearly six-hour trek on a crowded Greyhound bus to Van Wert, a small town in western Ohio. I was disappointed when I first arrived in the rural community surrounded by corn fields but felt reassured as I reunited with Tessie.

Tessie was working as a nutritionist and dietician for the Women, Infants, and Children Nutrition, Education, and Supplemental Food Program (WIC) in Paulding and Van Wert, Ohio. I planned to stay with Tessie for three months, but those months flew by and I realized that I wanted to stay in the United States long-term. There was a freedom here that I reveled in. I changed my visa from visitor to work status after gaining a work-visa sponsorship from a local school.

I had never aspired to move to the United States, but I had hoped to explore this land of milk and honey. Two of my best friends from my days working at Student Catholic Action (SCA) lived in the U.S., and my brother Diko had relocated to California in 1970. Several relatives were scattered around the country and I was anxious to see them, and all that this country had to offer.

I had nine women co-workers in SCA. I became close friends with one of them, Pauline Somoza-Manalo. We reconnected when I came to the States and remain friends to this day. In many ways, we are like sisters. We talk once a month on the phone – she lives in Frederick, Maryland – to exchange news about our lives. We also share our community projects and support each other in our spiritual growth. She is a friend for life.

Feli with Tessie, Ohio, Summer 1981.

> "These early months in the U.S. were a time of complete freedom."

These early months in the U.S. were a time of complete freedom. I didn't have home and child-rearing responsibilities. I toured the country, visiting places I had read about and seen in movies. I lived with Tessie for five months. And during that time, she and I became close friends with her boss, Linda Brown-Nash. Every weekend Linda would pick us up and we went to garage sales. She also introduced me to other American pastimes. Her parents treated us like their own daughters. Nearly every Sunday, they would invite us to dinner with their family. Their kindness helped alleviate some of my homesickness.

As I continued to nurture my prayer life which had always been a central part of me, I felt drawn to join the Sylvania Franciscans as a

Feli and Tessie Sebastian, Ohio, Summer 1981. This marked the first time Feli used an automatic washing machine.

Postulant[1] where I could explore my faith more deeply through study while living with the Sisters. I was born and raised Catholic and although I attended public school for most of my education, religion was an important part of my upbringing and culture. Nearly 80 percent of Filipinos were Catholic at the time.

For a year, I went back to what I had known – teaching. I worked as an assistant teacher at the Westside Montessori School in Toledo and lived with the Franciscan Sisters in Sylvania, an hour and a half northeast of where my sister lived.

I was barely living with the Sisters for three months when I had a major medical crisis. I woke up one morning feeling very, very tired and had a high fever. I missed work and wasn't able to attend to the community's daily activities and prayer. When Sr. Nancy found out, she said I should see a doctor. I told her I didn't have a doctor or health insurance. She informed the Mother Superior, Sr. Patrice, right away. Sr. Patrice immediately enrolled me in the community's health insurance and put me in the care of her personal physician. Dr. Geiger found a huge cyst in my right breast and it needed to be removed immediately. I was so worried since I didn't have enough money for the surgery and hospital expenses. Tessie didn't have the money to loan me either. I didn't want to call my parents to cause them worry and undue burden. I was shocked and in tears when Sr. Nancy told me not

---

[1] *"A Postulant is a person who makes a request to be admitted into a monastery or religious community and has formally moved in and begun to learn and live in a community while in the "asking" stage. The person takes classes to learn more about the order and the religious life and could participate in apostolic works of the order. It is the period before the novitiate." Aleteia.org*

to worry because the community would pay for it. Lucky for me, the cyst was benign. I was in the hospital for a few days. I received so many get well cards from the Sisters, many of whom I barely knew. When I came home to the convent, my room was decorated with a big banner that said, "Welcome back, Feli!" I felt so loved and accepted.

At the end of the school year, I resigned from my Montessori position and began to explore the life of a nun in earnest beginning my journey as a Novice² in the summer of 1982.

As I continued to delve into my faith, I joined the teaching staff at St. Francis School, run by the Sisters, as an assistant teacher and librarian. Since I did not have my teaching credentials yet in the States, Sr. Antoinette Dudek assigned me the task to serve as a companion to a seven-year-old African American girl with special needs. Her name was Deena³ and she was a sweet little girl who usually had a smile on her face and was dressed in colorful outfits with matching hair accessories that adorned her braids.

Feli at the convent.

I assisted her in everything from basic tasks to classroom learning. Sometimes we'd review individualized lesson plans, helping her sound

---

² *"A Novice (from the Latin for "new" or beginner) is a Postulant who has been formally and probationary received into a religious community in order to discern whether he or she is called to a vowed religious life. He/she enters the novitiate which is a period of 1-2 years of intense formation, study, and a deepening experience of prayer and self-awareness. Novitiate is the stage before the temporary professional vow." Aleteia.org*

³ *Name has been changed to protect privacy.*

out the alphabet and pronounce syllables. She didn't speak, but she could make sounds. I could see the frustration mount on her face when she wanted to say something but could not express her thoughts. Sometimes she would yell and other times she would hit her head on the table. My heart was broken whenever she had a meltdown. All I could do was try to soothe her.

This was the first time I had worked with a special-needs child and although the tasks I was given were simple, it was a challenging and demanding job. I was exhausted each afternoon as I walked the five minutes back to the Motherhouse where I lived. Each day I prayed for Deena's safety and for what the next day would bring both of us.

Every day for 10 months, I assisted Deena in her daily tasks, helping to educate and socialize her with her classmates. Although she was nonverbal, she expressed herself and would hold my hand to not only steady her step but to feel my presence. Near the end of the year, she reached out to me and said, "Feli." I was so startled. She repeated my name, "Feli," "Feli," "Feli" several times, clapping her hands. Tears sprung to my eyes as I hugged her and told her how proud I was of her. "Feli" was the first word she learned to say, and this made a lasting impression on me. We can all impact the life of one person.

After a year of assisting at the school, I entered the Novitiate with the Sylvania Franciscans to deepen my knowledge of the order's charism and spirituality and started my bachelor's degree in Religious Studies at Lourdes College (later named Lourdes University), changing my work visa to student status. I was granted a five-year stay in the U.S.

Winter 1981 – Respite

I was as excited as any kid to experience the wonder of snow for the first time. I made snow angels, built snowmen, and captured the beautiful flakes on my tongue.

During my second year of formation, I bonded with a woman named Penny who was also seeking the call of God to serve as a Sister in the community. She was from Minnesota and an only child. Like

Feli's first snow, 1981, at the Convent.

me, she already had an established career, but thought she was being called as a Sister. We were both discerning as we lived, studied, worked, and prayed about the next step in our lives.

As Novices, we were assigned specific tasks, either daily or weekly, and we joined a rotation of chores with other "seekers," women in formation discerning their vocations[4], and other Sisters. Penny and I were assigned to the kitchen, where we would wash and dry huge pots, pans, trays, and other cooking utensils. We ingratiate ourselves to Sister Verona, who was in charge of the kitchen and occasionally scored us some special treats, like an extra pop or a bag of chips.

One winter day, the snow was mounded high around the 89 acres of grounds surrounding the Motherhouse. We were both bored. Penny asked me if I had ever gone sledding. I replied, "No, we don't have snow in the Philippines."

Penny declared, "Then we should go!" She asked a couple Sisters if there were sleds on the grounds but came up empty-handed. Then with an impish smile she said, "Let's go to the kitchen."

I asked, "What are we going to find in there?"

She smiled and said, "Just follow me."

---

[4] *"There are usually three stages of Formation: 1. Aspirancy — becoming an aspirant means that one aspires to join a religious order. One continues with his/her regular life, while growing in his/her knowledge of and experiences with the order. It is a time of mutual discernment: the order with the aspirant and the aspirant with the order. 2. Postulancy, and 3. Novitiate." www.arlingtondiocese.org/vocation/for-women/how to become a nun*

The kitchen was closed, and all the Sisters were having an afternoon nap. We found our way in through an alternate passage and Penny headed straight to the shelves piled high with freshly washed pots, pans, and huge trays. She handed me one of the trays and said, "This is your sled," as she quickly grabbed another.

I wavered saying, "No, the Sisters might find out and we will get into trouble." She reassured me and said, "They're all sleeping. No one will find out and we are just borrowing them for a couple hours."

Holding the huge aluminum trays under our arms, we snuck out through the backdoor of the Motherhouse and into the backyard, which overlooks a wooded area. We found a small hill and Penny went first as I gave her a push. She went swooshing down the hill and walked back breathless and excited.

> "She went swooshing down the hill and walked back breathless and excited."

Next, it was my turn and I was scared. I envisioned losing my balance and tumbling down the hill.

Penny said, "Sit with your knees up; just hold on tight to the edge of the tray. When you start moving, just let the tray do its work. Don't jump off."

"Ready, go!" she exclaimed giving me a big shove.

And down I went with my heart in my throat, screaming with glee. Before I knew it, I was already at the bottom of the hill. I was laughing hard as I watched Penny get ready to slide down next and quickly raced back up to the top to give her a quick hug and push her down the slope. It was exhilarating to feel the wind on my face.

We were out in the cold for nearly two hours, taking turns pushing one another down the hill. Our hands and feet were numb from cold, our faces red from the wind and our throats hoarse from laughing. We were giggling as we returned the trays to the kitchen and made hot cocoa. We were never "found out," but the Sisters might have just overlooked our escapades.

I longed to enjoy all that winter had to offer and engaged in a few snowball fights in the yard surrounded by statues, benches, trees, and bushes shrouded in white. I enjoyed the peacefulness of the silent white flakes and my favorite time of day soon became early evening, when I'd take moonlight walks with my friend Sister Anna, a Franciscan from Poland who was also a student at Lourdes College.

The grounds of Lourdes College, Sylvania, Ohio.

Although I enjoyed the novelty of snow, at Christmas I missed my family intensely. I always played Santa on Christmas Day, passing out gifts and spending the day enjoying home-cooked specialties, such as menudo, kare-kare, pancit palabok, ube, and letche flan, that my mother and aunt would prepare.

The Christmas of 1981 was different.

My sister Tessie joined me at the convent, which was nearly deserted. Most of the Sisters and Novices were home with their families. We attended Christmas Eve Mass with the remaining Sisters and enjoyed a midnight snack afterwards. Christmas morning, Tessie and I awoke to exchange gifts and felt emptiness. We both missed our family and were overwhelmed with homesickness. International calls were so expensive and we both knew those precious minutes would just be a sob-fest. We ate a pre-bagged dinner from the kitchen and reminisced about Christmases in the Philippines. We missed the food, our family, and the traditions, but we knew we had to weather this to grow to be the women we were meant to be, the women our family wanted us to be. We went to bed in silence that night knowing that this was the first of several times our resolve would be tested.

Life in the convent

Novitiate Family, 1984. First row, from left, Srs. Lucilla, Nathaniel, Nancy, Faith. Second row, from left, Feli, Sr. Antoinette, Lorraine, Dorothy, and Penny.

I'm often asked what it was like while I discerned my path to the Sisterhood. Life in the convent began and ended each day in prayer. There was Mass at 7 a.m. and then breakfast, either together in the big dining hall of the Motherhouse or in individual apartments located on the grounds. At 8 or 8:30 a.m., everyone went to her ministry or job. The ministries varied depending on each Sister's skill set or talent. Most of the Sylvania Franciscans are teachers and nurses or worked in administrative healthcare. Others work in the parish, as assistants to parish priests, directors of children's religious education, or Rite of Christian Initiation of Adults (RCIA) programs. Others do simple jobs outside or within the convent, including working as cooks, retailers, or maintenance grounds and facility workers. Each ministry is important and is needed for the welfare of the people and the environment. The Sylvania Franciscans have two schools on their Motherhouse grounds. One is an elementary school, St. Francis, and the other is a college, now a university, Lourdes University. Many of the Sisters worked in both educational institutions.

As a Novice, I did not work but spent most of my time in studies and prayer. One day a week, I volunteered as a counselor for abused children at St. Anthony Villa, a state-licensed residential temporary home for abused children ages seven to 14 run by the Tiffin Franciscans. I also volunteered in the infirmary, where most elderly sisters reside. Most of them were ill and could not work anymore.

And in case you think all Sisters are serious and grouchy, you are wrong. This group was full of joy and was outright humorous and sometimes naughty. I remember an elderly Sister who was always quiet but who flashed a mischievous smile. She was thin and tall. She had no appetite and continued to lose weight while I and the other Novices were caring for her. The nurses would weigh her weekly to monitor her. Although she was as thin as a wisp, she was still weighing in at 100 pounds. We came to find out she was carrying paper weights in her pockets when they weighed her.

The Sister I loved and missed a lot once I left the convent was Sister Justin. She wore a white habit all the time and the only part of her body that was exposed was her face. She always had a beautiful smile that matched her eyes when they twinkled. Everything about her was holy. I noticed that her lips moved when she worked in the kitchen. Curious, I inched closer to her and I heard she was praying. She must have been in her 80s and was a cook in the Motherhouse kitchen for many years. She baked the most delicious chicken. She was always kind to me; always asking if I needed or wanted an extra serving of food. Sister Justin worked seven days a week, providing the community with meals three times a day. What a dedicated servant!

After work, the Sisters came home to their respective residences. Around 5 p.m., everyone gathered in the chapel for the evening prayer, then dinner. The remainder of the day was free time. Some prepared for their classes the next day, while others did leisurely things like watching television, singing, engaging in crafts with fellow nuns, or meeting with friends. During my first week I lived with them, I was surprised that they watched TV shows such as Falcon Crest and Dallas. I'm showing my age here! The first time I heard them discuss a character on Dallas, I thought they were talking about a nun from another residence!

Each group of nuns who live together has an option of whether to do another night prayer before bed or to pray privately. In the Novitiate House where I lived, we did a communal prayer once a week and took turns preparing the prayer. Fellow Novice and friend Penny and I were under the care and guidance of Sister Faith, Novice director, and Sister Nancy, Formation director, who saw to it that all our needs were taken care of as we discerned God's will for us.

As members of the Novitiate house, we also performed chores that were rotated monthly. As a Novice, you are assigned bathroom duties, among others.

> "When I left the convent, I was very sad as I was leaving the 'family' I had created over a three-year period. But I also felt free."

Changes from Vatican II in the Catholic Church were still being implemented when I joined the Sylvania Franciscans. Many Sister congregations were undergoing changes and focusing more on their founder's charisma. It was a tense time of change in the Catholic Church, and the religious communities were touched as well. As a Novice, we had a choice of whether to wear a full habit, a tunic covered by a scapular and cowl, as well as a veil. I chose to wear civilian clothes in hues of beige, brown, or white.

I followed the community's schedule: attending Mass, eating meals, praying, and socializing. The bulk of my time was spent in study – both delving into Scripture and doing homework – assisting the nuns in the kitchen or infirmary, and praying. This time is very important to a Novice as she discerns if she is called to the religious life. I also spent a lot of time reflecting, praying, and journaling. I had time to read books and discover great authors. It was during this time that I came across Basil Pennington's book Centering Prayer[5].

---

[5] *Pennington's book "Centering Prayer" was first published in 1980.*

During this time, I decided with the help of Sr. Philomena Agudo that although a spiritual and religious life were extremely important to me, I was not ready to dedicate myself to the Sylvania Franciscans. In the summer of 1984, I left the convent and decided my focus should be on helping others through counseling services.

When I left the convent, I was very sad as I was leaving the "family" I had created over a three-year period. But I also felt free. There was something inside me that yearned to grow and expand outside the confines of the convent. I knew I could have pursued my choice of career within the community and the Sisters would have supported me, but I was yearning for more. At that time, I did not know what it was. All I knew was that I had to free myself and follow the dictates of my heart.

These three years as a Postulant and a Novice helped me grow and develop into who I am today. It was the beginning of my self-discovery and rediscovery of God. As I discovered myself, I grew closer to God. Exploring the Sisterhood was so special, and it was a period of incredible personal growth. The biggest gift that I took away was prayer. It was within the walls of the convent that I discovered what Centering Prayer was and how I could experience His presence. I found myself hungry for prayer, hungry and thirsty for solitude. I could hardly wait to finish my chores or studying so I could embrace prayer. I sought Him wherever I was, whether in the woods, walking the grounds filled with flowers and birds, or on a moonlight stroll. Sunrise and sunset also brought me closer to Him as I was filled with awe at all God had provided. I also sought Him out in scripture, training myself to listen deeply to hear His voice and His message. Beyond Scripture and nature, however, I found God in silence. I sought Him in the Portiuncula chapel, in the deserted places on the convent grounds. This is where I can still find Him today, in those silent places where I can just be.

Transition from Teacher to Counselor – Leaving the Convent Behind

My desire to help others led me to work as a full-time counselor at St. Anthony Villa as I continued to work towards a bachelor's degree in Religious Studies at Lourdes College. However, for me to continue doing that, I had to earn a certification from a U.S. accredited institution even if I had already earned a Master's degree in Guidance and Counseling in the Philippines. I enrolled at the University of Toledo while continuing to finish my bachelor's degree in Religious Studies in Lourdes College.

In 1985, I graduated from Lourdes College and in the fall of the same year, I applied for a Ph.D. program at the University of Toledo. I resigned from my position at St. Anthony Villa and moved close to the Toledo campus to earn my doctorate in guidance and counseling. I was a graduate assistant in the Counselor Education and Human Services Department and a full-time student.

Years had passed and I had not returned to the Philippines. Little did I know, it would be nine years before I returned to my homeland. The journey back was expensive and time consuming, and there were so many new things jockeying for my time and attention. My time in Ohio was spent learning and adjusting to a new culture and language, government and religious practices, and shifting and sorting my priorities while still adhering to what I valued most in life.

I had always believed there were messages in every decision I made, and I tried to listen to and discern God's plan for me. It was during this time that I began attending religious retreats to help center myself. Under the guidance of Sister Germain in Sylvania, Ohio, I confessed that I was feeling guilty leaving my parents for so long to raise my younger siblings. I had found a job and was able to provide for myself, but I was anxious about shirking my responsibilities to my parents. Sister Germain helped calm my nerves by telling me to read Jeremiah 29:11: "For I know the plans I have for you, declared the Lord. Plans to prosper you and not harm you, plans to give you hope and a future." This passage became my inspiration whenever I was faced with worry.

Prayer continued to be an important part of my daily life. I would often think back to when I was four or five years old and I was in my paternal grandmother's town, San Miguel, visiting with my family. My mother nudged me out of my sleep at dawn to join the family in prayer. I dragged myself over to where the family was gathered near the entrance of the only bedroom in her small home. As I was still trying to acclimate to the darkness, rubbing my eyes to keep awake, I was drawn to the only light in the room coming from a single candle on the dresser. Atop the dresser stood statues and pictures of Jesus and Mary. That candle shone so bright that it illuminated the room as well as the hallway where we were gathered. I was in awe of its beauty. My grandmother led the prayer in our language, Tagalog, with my family saying the response. At the time, I did not know the prayer, but it had a musical quality that lifted my spirit. "Aba Ginoong Maria, napupuno ka ng grasya ang Panginoon Diyos ay sumasaiyo, bukod kang pinagpala sa babaeng lahat at pinagpala naman ang iyong anak na si Hesus." [Hail Mary, full of grace. The Lord is with thee. Blessed art thou amongst women, and blessed is the fruit of thy womb, Jesus.]

Whenever I struggle today to connect to the Lord, I envision that candle burning bright with my family gathered close. The silence and awe return. With renewed faith and vigor, I finished my coursework and had begun work on my dissertation in January 1987 when I got a call that would again shift my focus. I was 41 years old.

It was Bill, my long-time on-again, off-again American boyfriend of the past 20 years. He was living in India and invited me to visit him for a three-month sabbatical between finishing my coursework and starting my dissertation. I readily accepted.

We had met when I was 21 and we were both teaching at Xavier School near Manila. He was studying abroad at the time, then a Jesuit seminarian studying for the priesthood. He taught religion. We started out as friends who enjoyed debating and sparring on everything from religion to philosophy to politics. I admired his faith.

Through the years, we became pen pals and would visit each other on occasion. I was so enamored with him. We were both idealistic, and in hindsight, I was so very naïve.

He became disillusioned with the Catholic Church. Before he made his ordination to the priesthood, he wrote me and said he wasn't going through with it and wanted to explore different faiths. He wanted to explore life in an ashram in India. An ashram is simply a community of men and women who imitate the charisma or principles of its founder.

Bill visited me briefly in Manila before embarking on his travels. We lost touch for several years after that and took turns breaking off our relationship, only to find one another again. We were physically more apart than together, but my emotional attachment to him ran very deep.

When I moved to the States in 1981, I was resolute to begin an independent life on the other side of the world. Several years passed before I heard from Bill, but we found one another again. In 1987 when he asked me to join him in Auroville, a universal ashram near Pondicherry, Tamil Nadu in South India, I accepted. He claimed it was heaven on earth, a utopia of sorts where people lived in harmony and most things were bought through trade.

So, in June of 1987, I made the long sojourn to visit him. The trip was fraught from the beginning. I missed my connecting flight in New York, altering the timing of my multi-legged air travel. By the time I arrived in India at the Madras International Meenambakkam Airport, it was already 4 p.m. and Auroville was over a three-hour drive from that point. Bill told me before I left to take a taxi from the airport if my schedule was off. Remember, this was long before cell phones were used!

Luckily, the taxi driver spoke English and helped me load my luggage and the two large boxes of supplies I was transporting. As we left the airport, it began to darken. I had forgotten how after 5 p.m. dusk settles and darkens South Asia. I was beginning to worry about finding Auroville in the dark and felt helpless being in a foreign place with no way to communicate.

Most of the roads were rutted dirt paths. The only light we had were the headlights from the Maruti Suzuki we travelled in. We wandered around the countryside for hours. It was nearly midnight when I finally thought to look for something I could recognize – the temple called Matrimandir, which in Sanskrit means "Temple of the Mother."

I knew his home wasn't far from it, and at this point, the worst-case scenario would be to spend the night in the meditation center. We found the temple and

Feli creating pottery, India.

were turning around when the glare of the headlights rested upon a windmill. I knew I had found Bill's house. When he came out, I thought he was a mirage.

I spent three months in India living a very simple life. We visited various places and enjoyed the beauty and diversity of the large country. It was there that I learned to ride a bike at age 41, allowing me to navigate the countryside independently. I made pottery using a primitive wheel, rode an elephant in a reserve, explored temple ruins, and travelled on crowded buses to visit bustling markets.

Matrimandir, Auroville India, 1987 still under construction. The spiritual/meditation building was completed in 2008.

Auroville, which means the "City of Dawn," was a small village of about 200 people, located along the coast of the Bay of Bengal. The residents of Auroville rotated meeting in one of the community's houses every week to hold Zen meditation. Zen meditation and Centering Prayer, which I now practice, share several key points. They both seek to quiet the mind and refrain from the use of words, instead embracing the simple breath. However, their purpose is entirely different. Zen practitioners seek enlightenment, while those who practice Centering Prayer seek to commune with the Divine. While practicing Zen is a technique based on using transcendental meditation, Centering relies on building a personal relationship with God, a consent to be present in the Presence.

I met people from all over the world who came to live at Auroville – native Indians, Europeans, and Asians. There were few members from the United States. All those who I met were seeking solace from some kind of hurt. The village was created to realize human unity and its founder, The Mother, was inspired by Sri Aurobindo to create it. Residents and followers of the ashram believe in Sri Aurobindo's teachings. They were guided by the Bhagavad Gita, a 700-verse Sanskrit scripture that is part of the Hindu epic Mahabharata. One of its many teachings is the call for selfless action. Auroville is a self-contained community that has a huge temple, called Matrimandir, a school, office with a governing body, bakery, grocery, clinic, and other agencies to support its residents.

In many ways, an ashram is similar to a Catholic community such as Franciscans (followers of St. Francis) or Benedictines (followers of St. Benedict). These communities are also composed of men or women who imitate the charisma or principles of its founders.

Auroville is just one of hundreds of ashrams in India and so is Sri Aurobindo Ashram. The Sri Aurobindo building was where Sri Aurobindo and The Mother lived. It is a sort of shrine, much like Christians have shrines like the Shrine of Our Lady of Lourdes in Lourdes, France, where people come to pay homage and pray. It also is like a museum, displaying the things he and The Mother used, like books and clothes.

Feli on her bike, India, 1987.

As much as I enjoyed my time in India, as September drew near, I knew I had a choice to make. Bill wanted me to stay at the ashram with him and make a life there. He always said that if he would marry, it would be to me, but he came short of ever asking me to marry him. After I left, he wrote to me every week we were apart.

I knew in my heart that I wanted more. I wanted more for myself and I wanted to make a living as a counselor so I could help others while helping my family financially. Money gives you freedom and I wasn't ready to give that up. I knew that my home wasn't in India, but I felt certain Bill's future was there. I believe that Bill was not really made to be married, or in a steady relationship.

After I returned from India, I finished my dissertation and healed from my heartbreak. I missed Bill tremendously and not seeing him daily was difficult. My mother immigrated to the United States in April 1989 and having her by my side was a balm to my heart. She joined me and my father in my apartment.

Later that year, I moved to Bloomington, Illinois from Toledo and accepted a job in BroMenn Hospital's counseling department as a psychologist. My duties expanded to include working at Prairieview Center[6], a residential school for boys ages 12 to 21 who are deaf and who suffer from mental, emotional, and behavioral issues. I began working there in 1991 even though I didn't know sign language. For the first few years, I had an interpreter when I counseled the boys. Later, I took American Sign Language lessons and conducted counseling on my own.

I was their clinical psychologist for 20 years until I retired in 2011.

As a psychologist, I worked with clients from ages 5 to 65-plus in individual, group, couple, or family settings. I also worked with all kinds of abuse situations, and all types of personality disorders, including addiction and attention deficit problems. It was a challenging and demanding job and I was forced to devise a plan of self-care. Some steps I embraced included taking three-day weekends from Friday to Sunday and visiting the Abbey or a similar place for respite. I knew I needed to recharge after an emotionally and intellectually draining work week.

In all my counseling experiences, it was a two-way process where we both benefited. My clients helped me unknowingly as I guided them. I learned so much from them and I grew in wisdom as I walked with them in their pain and struggles. I always felt grateful for the trust they had in me to help them find solutions to their problems. I have many memorable stories of triumphs and victories as clients earned

---

[6] *The program closed in 2017.*

their sobriety, left abusive relationships, and turned tragedies into great causes.

Whenever I visited Prairieview Center, I always felt like I was entering a different world. In some ways, it was different. My clients are deaf, and half of the staff are deaf or are hard of hearing. Everyone was busy with their hands, signing their thoughts and feelings. Unless it was imperative to speak out loud, the staff had to sign to foster inclusion among those who could not hear. It looked different, but the atmosphere was filled with laughter and camaraderie. The staff, under the leadership of Mardi Klasen and later of Gayle Giusti, was so devoted to the boys and considered them family. Occasionally there was sadness and disappointment when one of the boys had to be hospitalized. There was a concern their co-residents might not be able to return. However, there was rejoicing when after a week or two, a client did return. Some of the boys would greet me at my car as I parked and jubilantly sign something like, "Johnny is back, Dr. Feli!"

Paul[7] was among my most challenging clients. Besides being deaf, he had witnessed violence and death in his family at a very young age. He was intelligent, but his trauma affected his ability to learn. He had flash backs and nightmares nearly every day and was put on heavy medications. When he had an episode, he was often restrained and/or hospitalized. He would tell me that he didn't want medication anymore. But for his and his co-residents' safety, he had to be medicated. For a year, he did not trust me and put me through several tests. Finally, when he realized I was never going to hurt or leave him, he softened. He began to cooperate more with the house rules, found a part-time job, and improved his school performance. When he turned 21, he aged out of the local program and was moved to the Northbrook, Illinois sister facility. Paul continues to write me around his birthday and holidays, giving me an update of his life and reminding me not to forget to send an occasional gift.

---

[7] *Name has been changed to protect privacy.*

In the spring of 1990, my parents joined me in Illinois from Ohio. My parents lived with me on and off for nearly 21 years. During this time, they would occasionally return to the Philippines for long visits with family and friends. In November 1990, I made my long-awaited trip back to the Philippines with my sister Tessie and brother Diko. My four unmarried siblings immigrated to the U.S. the following month, living in my small two-bedroom apartment. Soon my parents followed, and I had a full house. We soon realized that we needed bigger accommodations and in 1992 we moved to a bi-level home I bought on the east side of town. I often joke that my home was like an accordion; it would expand as needed. It was also around this time that I sought spiritual direction from Sister Audrey, a Benedictine[8] nun from St. Mary's Monastery in Rock Island, Illinois. She became my spiritual advisor and helped guide me as I grew in my faith.

The years went by and I continued to date Bill on and off, totaling 38 years. We had been emailing and calling each other more frequently and regularly since he returned to the States in 2000 to care for his ailing mother. Prior to that move, we had taken a 10-year hiatus from one another. He was still very charismatic, and I could feel myself being pulled back to him. I was dazzled by his goodness and his faith. At the time, he was working in prison ministry in California. I think

---

[8] *The Benedictines, officially the Order of Saint Benedict (Latin: Ordo Sancti Benedicti, abbreviated as OSB), are a monastic Catholic religious order of monks, nuns, and laypeople who follow the Rule of Saint Benedict.*

that's what always touched my heart – that he was always doing the work of God. While I was feeling high and excited with him being back in my life, I was also feeling tired of the uncertainty of my future.

In 2006, I decided to meet him one final time to find out exactly what his plans were for us. When he said he had no plans for us to get married, I told him I wanted to move on with my life without him. As I left California, he begged and begged for us to stay in touch as friends. I did not have the heart to say no.

Preparing for my flight back to Illinois, I stopped by the airport gift shop looking for something to read on the long flight. As I was browsing, a book fell off the shelf near me. As I bent down to pick it up, I noticed the title, "How to Break Your Addiction to a Person"[9]. Realization hit me like a ton of bricks.

I bought that book and read it in full before we landed. I felt so embarrassed and stupid. I had been a psychologist for 17 years and I didn't recognize the signs that I was poorly attached and addicted to a person I loved. It was an unhealthy relationship between two good people. I had thought that one could only be addicted to something bad, like drugs or alcohol. I didn't know I was so addicted to him because I was narrowly focused on what I wanted, and thought was good for me. I ignored a lot of red flags. I was resolute from that point on to be "sober".

I followed the book's 12-step program diligently. I prayed hard to God to strengthen me. I recognized my weakness and I knew I needed the Higher Power, someone bigger than my attachment to help me remain sober because, for nearly 40 years, I was a slave to my addiction. By then, I was 60 years old. I learned to recognize my triggers of addiction to Bill. Although, he continued to write me, I no longer clutched onto his words, "BUT if I were to get married, it would be to you." And each time I was tempted to go back to him, I would stop

---

[9] *"How to Break Your Addiction to a Person" by Howard M. Halpern*

and cherish how wonderful it was to feel *FREE*. I forgave myself and Bill. I accepted myself, broken but still God's Beloved.

The last I have heard, Bill returned to India. I returned to my life. It wasn't easy, but I knew then what would make me happy, and I definitely knew what made me unhappy.

Now, when I hear from women who are attached to relationships and men who drag them down, I have greater empathy. I can relate to an unhealthy relationship. I really understand experientially what attachment is. I also know that you can free yourself.

4 BRANCHING OUT

Eager to start a practice of my own – something I had aspired to since I began graduate school – I quit BroMenn in 1997 and began seeing patients in my private practice. I knew I would have more freedom and flexibility with my own practice, and I could establish more in-depth relationships with my clients as I saw fit.

However, setting up a private practice was daunting. With help from an accountant and a lawyer, I navigated my way through the entrepreneurship basics, ensuring I was a preferred provider with most local insurance carriers. I also traded services for rent in the House of Prayer on Center Street in downtown Bloomington. I saw several students at a local Catholic school free of charge and in turn, had my rent covered for several years.

I also had assistance from former coworkers who had gone solo. At the time, BroMenn Hospital (now Carle Advocate BroMenn) was undergoing a major reorganization that included changes in the counseling department, resulting in larger caseloads. I felt it was the right time to make the switch.

It was a stressful and busy time. I was juggling my career, living with and taking care of my aging parents, while building Labyrinth House, a non-profit for women in need I had started in 2004.

Centering Prayer

Prayer continued to guide me. I began my day with a Centering Prayer practiced by the Benedictines. For several years prior, I had dedicated myself to a Benedictine prayer group, and in 1998, I became an Oblate, a layperson of the Benedictine Sisters of St. Mary Monastery.

One way we practice and share our faith is to meet once a month at a local church to study a reading and focus on one of the Benedictine virtues – love, humility, prayer, solitude, leisure, obedience, discipline, hospitality, community, and forgiveness.

According to the World Community for Christian Meditation, "Apart from the prayer and community there is the creative venture of living out the spirituality of St. Benedict in our daily lives. Primarily that means applying it to the context of family, relationships, leisure time and the workplace, living a life of prayer and meditation through the commitments, opportunities and responsibilities of our life.

" 'The tools for good works,' as St. Benedict calls them, need to be used creatively. The way we live out our Oblation and calling is unique for each person." [10]

The Benedictines believe in balancing prayer, work, and play, a constant challenge for me! I really feel a dissonance when I am out of balance. To help me stay on track with "The Rule," the Benedictine guide, I follow St. Benedict's teaching: "Prefer nothing whatever to Christ." It dictates the way I live my life while I listen with the ear of my heart.

Even with my spiritual practices and deep faith anchoring me, a series of events and build-up of past stress eventually brought me to my breaking point in 2006. Although I still sought out the Lord to guide me during these challenges, I found myself getting angry. I was frustrated, sad, and disheartened. I questioned my faith and Jesus and their relevance in my life. I was still in the process of releasing myself

---

[10] *https://www.wccm.org/content/becoming-oblate*

from my past relationship with Bill and I was working around the clock.

I would start every day with my Centering Prayer in a small room I had dedicated as a Prayer Room in my home. However, nothing but anger spewed from my mouth. My heart held mounting frustration and despair. I wailed and lamented. One day, I stepped out of the circle of what I was taught, believed, and experienced as a Catholic. I did not want to be Catholic; worse, I did not want to believe in God, or in anything.

I felt I was going through the motions, trying to live and work every day, but inside, I felt all dried up. I was emotionally and spiritually spent. Soon, the physical repercussions of my distress would manifest.

An itching, burning, scaly rash began to take over my body from my collarbone to my toes. No amount of lotion and cream would abate it. Visits to the dermatologist were futile.

My misery continued for nearly two years. I was in a physical and spiritual crisis that was unrelenting. No kind of treatment would heal me or bring relief. I used all kinds of ointments and pills, even subjecting my body to phototherapy where the body is exposed to ultraviolet light for its healing effects. But the rashes stayed, clinging to my skin like leeches.

I told Father Marion, my spiritual advisor at the time, "I don't want to believe anymore. I don't want to be Catholic anymore. I just want to step out."

Father Marion was so calm. He simply said, "I'll pray for you and if you come back to the circle, you come back. If you don't, you don't."

I couldn't believe he wasn't upset. I said, "You're not concerned?" He replied, "I think it's His will for this to happen. Jesus is with you. The Lord is with you."

To add to my heartache, my sister Girlie, a nurse who had immigrated to Toronto, Canada in 1997, was diagnosed with cancer in the fall of 2009. I began to travel to Canada nearly every other week over the next five months to help care for her before she eventually succumbed to the disease.

From left, Feli and sister Girlie in Door County, WI, 2004.

While in Canada supporting Girlie, I had a terrible car accident. I was the driver and two of my sisters were with me. Although no one died or was severely injured in the crash, I felt a lot of guilt. The night of the accident, I felt so alone and abandoned, despite assurances from my family that I did nothing wrong. It was also that night when I finally gave up fighting God.

I cried myself to sleep. I awoke sometime later, and I began praying in earnest. During that prayer, I had a vision. I saw myself at the bottom of a pit or dungeon, much like I had seen in an earlier pilgrimage to the Holy Land. I felt the presence of Jesus in the pit and I said to God: "I am tired of fighting you. I surrender. Do whatever you want with me. You have taken everything already away from me." Then I felt a warmth…a Presence. And I knew who it was.

From that point on, I had a peacefulness envelop me.

I returned to the United States and although I was still battling the rashes externally, the internal peace persisted.

I continued to research treatments while I was trying yet another recommended cream by a dermatologist. I came across a website that claimed Dead Sea salt would calm rashes. I was grasping at anything, so I ordered it. The day it arrived, I soaked in the Dead Sea salt and I again felt that sense of peace wash over me. The scales started to heal. Today, I don't have a single scar and remain rash-free.

That was a turning point. I began to reconnect with God and practice my faith again. I had hope. After my sister Girlie died in 2010, my parents were devastated, particularly my father, who was in failing health already. I knew in my heart that had I not reconnected with God before her death, I would have experienced greater melancholy and even greater depression. It was very hard and painful, of course, but I had a greater sense of acceptance at that point. Me and my sister Tessie were at Girlie's side when she drew her last breath. She prepared me and my family to accept her impending death by writing the phrase, "All shall be well" in her letters to us.

I've concluded that I had to undergo that miserable body-length rash ordeal to grow closer to God, to rid myself of the "junks" in my life. It was a cleansing of sorts, albeit a difficult and painful one. Losing Girlie made me refocus and redouble my efforts to create Labyrinth, my fledgling non-profit. She was a strong supporter and with every move I made to enrich these women's lives, I knew I was doing so in part to honor her.

> "During that prayer, I had a vision. I saw myself at the bottom of a pit or dungeon, much like I had seen in an earlier pilgrimage to the Holy Land. I felt the presence of Jesus in the pit and I said to God: 'I am tired of fighting you. I surrender.'"

This trial has led me to be more empathetic with those who are in the process of releasing toxins from their life – whether that's other people, drinking, or drugs. Although I still get frustrated, I stop and tell myself that I, too, was in that same situation. We're all in the process of letting go of something.

5 REAWAKENING

At the request of my parents, my youngest brother Ray and I began preparing to move them back to the Philippines in November 2010. They would join my brother Jovi, a priest who lived in the church rectory in Bulacan.

I was 63 years old and for the first time in 21 years, I would be living on my own again. I was not afraid. I had lived alone for 10 years before my siblings and parents immigrated to the States. However, my sister Gelly was concerned, as was my cousin Linda. On their insistence, they enrolled me in Match.com, a dating service. I was leery about it. I'm old-fashioned and conservative and this seemed wild to me.

I said, "I'm not looking for a husband!" Linda, who was really instrumental in this said, "No, we're just looking for a friend for you, so that when you want to go see a movie or go for a walk or a concert, you have someone to go with."

I relented, all the while thinking, "You just want to get rid of me because I'll be tapping on your door saying, 'Do you want to meet at the movies?'"

The dating service was fun because it was something new. It was entertaining at first as I browsed through the suggestions Match.com sent, enjoying sharing every move I made with my cousin and my sister.

Finally, in early May, I came upon someone who sent me a "Wink." I'm not sure if I winked first or he did, but I started talking to a man named Jim. Since our communication was via email, I felt safe, as I could keep my distance. However, I got scared when it advanced to meeting him in person. I was ready to back off, but Linda encouraged me to "just try it." And so I did.

Ironically, that week I was meeting another match who was also named Jim. I met up with Jim #1 for a golf date. I wasn't much of a golfer, but he said he'd teach me the basics. Although he was a nice man, he was not really ready to start a new relationship, as he was still grieving over a previous one. I did not think it was a good match.

So, on to Jim #2. We decided to meet at Panera. Ever careful, I followed the Match.com rules by the book and told him my name was "Adrienne," which happens to be my middle name.

Linda agreed to sit nearby at the restaurant in case I needed to make a quick escape. She was also there for moral support.

On my drive to the restaurant, I kept telling myself, "You're not Feli; you're Adrienne." I didn't want to slip up on something so basic! Jim was already there when I arrived. We greeted each other and sat down. Nearly 10 minutes later, my cousin walked in and sat down behind us.

I thought we'd meet briefly, but Jim and I began talking and soon, over an hour had slipped by. My cousin texted me that she was leaving and to report back to her immediately. Jim and I had a lot in common, so that first hour tumbled into the next.

Afterwards, I drove to meet my anxious sister and cousin. Linda gave him high marks for what she overheard and deemed that he looked dignified and well-dressed, saying, "I think you're safe if he asks for another date." We hadn't discussed seeing each other again, but I hoped that we would.

My phone rang later that week and Jim asked if we could meet again. We met for lunch at a local Italian restaurant where we split the bill. He was as unsure of the "dating rules" as I was, and we laughed about the angst that bill paying caused.

It was on that date that I told him I had something to reveal: "My name isn't Adrienne. It's Feli," I confided.

He also said he had something to share: "I am not yet divorced. It's in the process. It will be final in two, maybe three months."

I was disappointed. This was a deal-breaker for me. "Well, in that case, this is the end," I said. "I don't want to continue dating you." I knew he was interested in me, and I was interested also – so it would really be insincere to say, "We'll be friends."

But he was insistent, begging to continue to see one another and before I even returned to the house, I had several voice messages from him. I finally responded that when his divorce was final and if he was still interested, he could contact me. If I was still single, we could begin dating again.

So we stopped communicating. I really admired him for respecting my wishes. "There will be more matches," I thought. And there were, but I didn't meet anyone special.

Three months later, Jim emailed me. He said, "The papers are signed. Can we resume seeing each other?"

I agreed, and we met at the senior center where I enjoy line dancing. He was totally out of his element, but I knew he was trying as I checked him out in the big mirror that reflected half of the room.

We continued dating for the next several months. We saw each other about once a week since he lived about an hour west of me in his hometown, Peoria. One thing that really touched me about Jim was his respect of my schedule and the time I dedicate to attending Mass. Eventually, he started asking if he could attend church with me.

Soon I was preparing my parents for their big move back home to the Philippines. We were hosting a send-off party for them at my brother Ray's house that November. This was the perfect time to introduce Jim to my large family.

The whole family was anxious to meet this mystery man. Everybody was at the party. But, alas, no Jim!

My siblings were all asking me, "Where is he? Does he have a phone? Why don't you call him?" It was unheard of for me to call him – I'm old-school – but they were harassing me, so I did.

I picked up the phone, and I just said, "Where are you?" And I didn't even realize I didn't say who I was. I hung up. I was so upset that he didn't show up.

The next day, I went to Mass. When I returned home from church, I had nine messages on my cell phone, asking me, "Where is the party?"

Jim said he was sitting in my driveway and the house was dark. He was so confused.

The next time the phone rang, I picked it up and said, "No, the party was yesterday!"

He had the date wrong.

I was still angry, but he was so apologetic. He asked, "Can I still come? I have a gift for your mom." The party was also in celebration of my mother's 90th birthday later that month.

I said, "Wait. I'll ask my mom if you can come." I was punishing him by making him wait just a bit.

When I called my mom she said, "Of course he can come; he's driven a distance!" This nearly knocked me over. In the past my mom was always so judgmental saying, "No, no, no! Don't get married," or, "Don't have a boyfriend." But she was so nice to him!

So, I called him back and said, "Okay, you can come." In a few minutes, he knocked at my door carrying beautiful orchids for my mom.

My dad was holed up in their bedroom. At that time, he was very depressed and would hardly get up for meals. I said, "Dad, did you have dinner yet?" He replied, "No, I don't want to eat."

I said, "You'd better eat. Don't you want to see the guy who is courting me?" In the Filipino culture, it's more courting than dating.

He sprung up! When my dad entered the room, he started sizing Jim up. Then they sat down and talked, and really seemed to get along. Jim knows how to work with the oldies.

My mom suggested we go to my cousin's house to join the rest of the group for dinner. Everyone loved Jim and I surprised myself by falling for him even more. By my standards, our relationship evolved very quickly. Later that month, I was off to the Philippines to settle my parents back with my brother Jovi and I missed Jim while I was away.

However, I confided to my cousin Linda that perhaps our relationship was moving too fast. I asked her, "When do you really know you've met the person you want to spend the rest of your life with?"

I thought we should date at least a year before we get engaged. She laughed and said, "Ate, Ngayon na," which is Filipino for "It's time." And then she added, "You have no more time to wait. You are old."

Which is true. If you are in your twenties, you have time. I was 63! But she said, "If in your heart you feel that you found him, what's the reason for waiting?" Ever hesitant I said, "There might be something else I haven't found out yet."

> "Once I returned from three weeks in the Philippines, I knew that I had found 'The One.'"

Once I returned from three weeks in the Philippines, I knew that I had found "The One." A couple days after the 2011 New Year, Jim proposed. I was overwhelmed with joy.

I had a sore throat, so I couldn't shout, "Yes!" I could barely speak, but he understood my answer.

Afterwards, one of the first things he said to me was, "I want us to get married in the Philippines because I want your parents to see you get married." Before we began planning the long-distance wedding, however, I said he had to write or call my dad and ask for his blessing. It's a Filipino tradition, no matter how old someone might be.

Jim wrote them a letter, but before they received it, I was bursting to call and tell them our news. My mom was so uncharacteristically relaxed and said, "Well, if you feel this is it, then I give you my blessing."

However, my dad was a different story. He said, "You're already old, and you will still get married?" And then he added, "How sure are you?"

When I reached out to my eldest brother Jovi, I asked if he would marry us. He replied, "Of course I will." I think this helped pave the way for my dad's eventual blessing.

Jim worked at Caterpillar in Peoria for 35 years. He had two adult daughters, Jennifer and Ashley, from his previous marriage. For us to get married in the Catholic Church, he had to apply for an annulment[11]. The process could take up to three years and I asked him if he was ready for that kind of wait. After some thought, he said he was, and I was even more impressed with his respect for my traditions and my beliefs. We both knew we were worth waiting for.

Jim's annulment was fast-tracked due to a technicality. We began planning for an October wedding in the Philippines.

However, our plans to marry were halted when my dad had a heart attack March 17 and died. I accompanied my family and returned to the Philippines for his funeral. Afterwards, there was a big discussion around if I could marry that same year. According to the Filipino tradition it is customary not to hold a family wedding in the same year as a parent's death.

My siblings were split on our upcoming wedding. Some said, "What are you waiting for? Dad knew you were going to get married. He gave his blessing."

Yet others were saying, "Well, maybe this is providential. Maybe you need a little bit more time to think about whether you're going to go through with this marriage."

I sought out my dad's sister's advice. Aunt Ote said flat out, "Go ahead. Your dad knew you were going to get married. He's in a different place now, and in that place, he understands better."

My brother Diko added, "There are too many sorrows. We want more joy now. Go ahead – get married." Diko was right. In a fairly

---

[11] *According to the United States of Catholic Bishops, "An annulment is a declaration by a Church tribunal (a Catholic church court) that a marriage thought to be valid according to Church law actually fell short of at least one of the essential elements required for a binding union."*

short time span, we had lost my sister Girlie, Jim's cousin and his mother, my dad, and soon after, my Aunt Ote.

However, I still needed time for reflection, When I returned to the U.S., I went on a week-long retreat at St. Bede's Abbey to pray about it and process all the events that had culminated. Abbot Philip helped me explore my thoughts and feelings.

I thought about our Filipino tradition of mourning. Filipino women mourn for their beloved dead by wearing black dress and men wear a black ribbon on their lapel for one year. No one is allowed to wear a bright colored outfit. My favorite color red was banned. No one is allowed to host or attend parties, or anything that calls for fun, because it runs contradictory to grieving. One must demonstrate the sorrow one feels. However, I believe this tradition is mostly an act. My grief is personal, and it is solely my business.

I knew in my heart that I was sad and missed my dad. But I am alive, and I didn't want to be "buried" with him. God is the God of the living, not the God of the dead. Who would I be disappointing if I got married within this grieving period? I knew my siblings meant well, but I also knew that it was my happiness at stake.

From left, sisters Gelly, Feli, Tessie and Aline, Oct. 7, 2011.

I concluded that I am not responsible for anyone's feelings but my own. I have no obligations to please anyone and I am responsible for my decisions and the consequences of my actions. All my life, I had put aside my choices because of my family – because I loved them, and they came first. Selfish or not, I felt strongly that I must take control of my future.

I could not think of any credible reason to delay our wedding. All the other barriers, such as Jim's annulment, were resolved. I also believe that God is a merciful God. He only wants us to be free and happy. I don't know why he took my dad at this time, but perhaps my dad knew that I would be okay, that someone was now here to take care of my heart.

In the end, I followed my heart and felt at peace with my decision. I decided that yes, we would marry that October in 2011, but we would marry in the United States and my mother would attend. However, as October approached, my 90-plus-year-old mother's health was too frail. Her doctor advised against the long travel. Jovi was not able to marry us because he was the primary caregiver to our mom, and he did not want to leave her behind.

We were heartbroken, as was she, but the wedding proceeded at Holy Trinity Church in Bloomington on October 7, which happens to be the Feast Day of The Holy Rosary. We were married by Abbot Philip Davey, Order of St. Benedict at St. Bede Abbey. Some of the monks of the Abbey sang during our wedding day Mass. Our wedding entourage, from the flower girls to the sponsors, were members of our families. Ashley, Jim's daughter, was our candle sponsor. My sister Gelly was my maid of honor; my sisters Tessie and Aline were my bridesmaids. My youngest brother Ray was our best man. Judi, Jim's sister, was our reader. My brother Diko walked me down the aisle.

We had about 150 people in attendance and we videotaped the entire thing. We honeymooned in the Philippines, where we shared the wedding experience with my mother by watching the video more than a few times. My mother and Jim really bonded on that three-week trip. We spent a lot of time visiting family and Jim finally got to meet my brothers Jovi, Toots, and Ermie.

Jim is very patient, playful, kind, and considerate. He's also down-to-earth, practical, and easy to forgive. I think there's a difference in marrying older than marrying younger. I think if you marry younger, you grow together. Granted, that is if it's a good relationship. But when you marry older, you're already set in your ways. This was especially true with me. For 65 years, I was on my own and very independent. But Jim was very patient; he understood when I needed time or space. He also understood how to inject some playfulness into our relationship.

> "The 'noes' in reality were really 'not yets.' The time was not yet ripe for me to meet Jim, the 'Real One.' When he finally came, it was the perfect time."

From such an early age I had so much responsibility. It was sometimes hard for me to be free and have fun. All my life, my role has been the giver – to my family, to friends, to everyone. I didn't know any other way. When Jim came into my life, it was a total reversal of what I was used to and familiar with. I became the receiver and he was the giver. It took a while for me to get used to it, and sometimes it still feels awkward to be on the receiving end of care. But Jim says, "You've always taken care of others. It's your turn now to receive."

Feli and Jim, October 7, 2011.

At times I think Jim and I are so different, and we are in a lot of ways, but we are alike in the ways that count. We share the same values and beliefs. We honor each other. We take care of each other. Jim converted to Catholicism through the Rite of Christian Initiation for Adults (RCIA) in 2012 after we were married. He now shares my faith, which I really am grateful for.

One's relationship with God is so personal – you must go about it your own way. I consider Jim God's gift to me. And I believe it even when we have conflicts or when I feel disappointed on some issues. I accept Jim is not perfect. He is a gift, but not a perfect gift. No one is perfect. I'm convinced we were put together to help one another reach our potentials.

Just like timing was the key in every phase and development of Labyrinth, so was my love life. For as long as I can remember, I always wanted to be married – to be loved by "someone special." I prayed about it and nothing happened for the longest time. My dream that my relationship with Bill would end in marriage looked hopeless, so I ended it. I felt God was deaf to my prayer. When the "Real One" didn't arrive after Bill, I abandoned the idea of marriage. I resigned myself to remain single the rest of my life. And just as I gave up on marriage, Jim appeared. It was similar to the many "noes" I received from other organizations to assist Labyrinth. The "noes" in reality were really "not yets." The time was not yet ripe for me to meet Jim, the "Real One." When he finally came, it was the perfect time. I was clean from my attachment to Bill and all my responsibilities to my parents and family were finished. I was free to pursue my own happiness. Jim's timing couldn't have been more appropriate.

Jim and Feli celebrate an anniversary.

For the next four years, my mother continued to live in the Philippines with Jovi. In November 2015, Jim and my siblings and I returned home to celebrate her 95th birthday. When the rest of the family returned to the States, I decided to stay and take care of my mother through the end of March. I had a wonderful three months with her where I cooked all her favorite foods, played bingo, watched movies, enjoyed concerts, and attended to her needs. My fondest memory was our intimate talks of her child-rearing years with the ten of us and her life with my dad.

She was content, but she missed my dad so much. During my stay, she became ill and struggled to recover from a bout of pneumonia. We lost her after a two-week battle with the disease. All my siblings returned to the Philippines to be by her side during her final days.

My mother, Felisa Sarmiento Sebastian, died February 25, 2016. Sadly, my younger brother Ermie died just three months later.

Felisa and Feli, Christmas 2015. Sebastian's Dream House, where Felisa enjoyed played Santa, 2015.

6 HEALING

When I returned to the U.S., I was still reeling with grief. I joined a small group of senior musicians called The Grannies Band. The concept really intrigued me. Growing up, I was told rock and roll was bad, and only listened to classical and jazz music. I wanted to express and expand myself. Seven of us women joined together to form the band. The band was founded by ISU music professor Dr. Kim McCord in 2016. She started the band after hearing about the popular Finish Grannies, a musical group of senior women between the ages of 65 to 84 who lost their spouses. Once, we even synced our band with theirs via satellite and played together. I played the keyboard and flute, which I learned to play through the Figure Notes system, the same music program I would later use to help teach music to the women of Labyrinth that was led by Illinois State University music students Sam Kubil and Kaitlyn Bauman. Our local group played together a little over a year and then disbanded when the number of practices and commitment got to be overwhelming.

Although I officially retired from my clinical practice in 2011, I continue consultations with the Social Security Disability Determination Department, the Tribunal of the Diocese of Peoria, and the Quality, Timeliness, Customer Service on Veterans Affairs.

Central Illinois Grannies Band and their mentors.

PART TWO
The Birth of Labyrinth

7 INSPIRATION

It could have been me. That's ultimately why I shifted Labyrinth House from an outreach organization for homeless and disadvantaged women to a home and outreach program for formerly incarcerated women in the heartland of Illinois. Who knows what small daily decisions each of us make that could lead us to the other side of those bars? Different choices, different upbringings, and often a series of bad circumstances ultimately placed them on one side of the enclosure and me on the other. These thoughts all raced through my head as I waited for our first prisoner interview at Logan Correctional Center, some 30 miles north of Springfield in August 2004. Theresa*[12] arrived, nervous and fidgeting, her long hair swept up in a ponytail and her knee feverishly bouncing. She sat across from me and began to share her story. She detailed abuse, drugs, and desperation – a story I would later hear repeated in many forms throughout the years. She knew she was ready to begin navigating her way back to the community. And I was ready to help.

---

[12] *Throughout Part Two, names denoted with * have been changed to protect the privacy of our clients.*

8 LABYRINTH IS BORN

It was the summer of 2004 and along with my growing professional duties as a psychologist in private practice, I was also the primary caretaker for my elderly parents who lived with me, and a financial supporter of a few of my younger siblings. To help center myself, I habitually practiced "quiet days" at St. Bede Abbey in Peru, Illinois about 60 miles northwest of my home in Bloomington.

I began visiting the abbey in 1999 one weekend each month to find peace and feel more connected to my faith. My days consisted of rest, prayer, journaling, and reflection. I also met with my spiritual advisor Father Marion, who helped me with discernment and prayer. I wanted to be sure that what I was doing with my life was consistent with what I was called to do.

It was during one quiet reflection in the summer of 2004 that I felt called to establish an outreach program for women in need in Bloomington. At first, I thought, "What? I am not prepared for this. I have my own counseling practice, and so many responsibilities. No, I am not ready." But the idea kept creeping back.

St. Bede Abbey, Peru, Illinois.

Later that summer, I returned to the abbey. I confided this calling to Father Marion. He simply said, "Let's pray about it." I nearly wanted to grab my words back because even with his support, I didn't feel ready to take on such a challenge.

Ironically, around this time a friend in Nashville reached out. Eileen, a member of the Religious Sisters of Mercy, shared with me a project she had started. She named it House of Mercy, a transitional home for mothers recovering from drug and alcohol addictions[13].

After financially supporting House of Mercy for several months and learning more about their program, I thought maybe I could replicate their program here in Illinois. I started browsing the internet, oftentimes until the early morning hours. I was slowly uncovering how to start a non-profit and how to establish a board of directors.

When I first had the concept for this service, I was not focused on helping formerly incarcerated women. As I developed a board of directors who would guide the formation of what is now Labyrinth Outreach Services, our mission was to serve single, homeless women suffering from addiction, who have a mental illness, or are in poverty – and often all three.

I began working with Karen Zangerle, Executive Director of McLean County's PATH (Providing Access to Health) program, a community resource people turn to when they are seeking help in human services. With her assistance, we formed a Task Force in 2004 to study the viability of the program I had in mind. We met every other week for nine months to draw up a mission statement, vision, policies, and procedures.

We also worked to establish a board of directors and our first Labyrinth Board met in September 2005. People from all professions came together at that first meeting – lawyers, accountants, social workers, and university employees.

The board continued to meet and develop ideas, sharing our vision with those we met.

---

[13] *Sadly, after 10 years in operation, House of Mercy closed its doors in 2008.*

In the meantime, I gave presentations and found ways to raise funds to add to the seed money for the organization. I taught myself how to write grants and asked, or rather begged, for money from my family and friends. On my birthday, I asked my family to donate towards Labyrinth instead of giving gifts to me. My youngest sister, Aline, was our first donor. My family continued to support Labyrinth. In 2019 my youngest brother Ray sponsored a fundraising cookout in his backyard called "Crazy Hats." Guests came in their funny, weird hats. Prizes were awarded to the craziest one.

From left, Kevin and my brother Ray.

While setting up Labyrinth, I recognized right away that my response and attitude towards the challenges I faced determined the next steps I would make. Just like walking the labyrinth, if I made a wrong turn and ended up in a dead end, I felt challenged and discouraged. In fact, I thought many times about abandoning the project. Why did I continue? I do not know the exact reason, but I felt I could not leave. There was always this encouraging voice to keep going, either in my head or from friends. Usually after taking a break at the abbey, I would feel a surge of energy and a sense of direction. The monks kept me on task, especially after many long conversations with my spiritual advisor Father Marion. Along the way I often said, "You cannot leave me now, Lord. There must be something worthwhile in doing this because You have led me this far."

It was also around this time when I changed my attitude about failure. I focused on the positives I gained and how I could learn from my mistakes. I read what other dreamers did, how they turned around negative events, who they sought for strength and inspiration. I also stopped blaming myself for any wrong moves I might have made.

We had a small amount of seed money from St. Patrick Church of Merna. Our goal was to establish the organization as a 501(c)(3), guaranteeing non-profit status. We hired a lawyer and an accountant to submit our application.

Unfortunately, it came back stamped, "Denied!" I was crushed. We had used $3,000 – all of our seed money – to establish our status and now we were back to square one. I decided to revise the paperwork myself with some help from a dear friend who had started a Bloomington non-profit called Recycling Furniture for Families. We resubmitted the application. Luckily, we were granted non-profit status later that year and were legally declared a 501(c)(3) organization on June 14, 2005.

In the meantime, Karen Zangerle connected me to Safe Harbor, an organization that runs a homeless shelter for men in downtown Bloomington. They were interested in partnering with us to provide temporary housing for women in need. Our group continued to look at houses and apartment buildings to accommodate our program, but to no avail. We had little money and couldn't find a grant to support our mission. I was feeling defeated. The Town of Normal even agreed to lease us property at one dollar a year if we built our group home on their lot near an abandoned Sailors and Soldiers Home that had closed in 1979. Unfortunately, we had $6.95 in the bank at the time and no way to raise enough funds for a building project. We had grants in the works, but nothing had come through yet.

To add to our hurdles, the government's funding model changed, and it was no longer willing to fund temporary housing for the homeless. Instead the government wanted to focus on funding permanent housing solutions. This was in direct opposition to our temporary housing mission and the Labyrinth Board would not approve this change to permanent housing. Our goal was – and continues to be – to move residents to independence.

Four years went by, during which time we developed and adapted our mission and started looking for a house for our clients – or those we hoped to serve. In the meantime, I shared my office, phone, and mailbox, enabling Labyrinth House to begin operations without a true home.

As the members of the board of directors dwindled, we'd recruit new members. Some stuck and others didn't. The board was like a revolving door for a while.

One of the early lessons I learned was to be flexible, to rebuild, to start all over when the pieces did not fit.

Father Marion counseled me about the board and simply said I should choose board members with more diligence and commitment. I firmly believed that Labyrinth was not my project, but God's, and followed Father Marion's advice. In 2008, we caught a break.

Through what I like to call divine intervention, I ran into a woman I had worked with several years before in the counseling department at BroMenn Hospital. Mary Campbell, a social work professor at Illinois State University, would become the energizing force we needed on the board. She began serving as the board's co-president with me in June 2008. Mary would also help me spearhead a shift in our organization's mission and find our much sought-after, but ever-elusive house.

My hunch that Mary was God-sent was affirmed over and over. First, I needed someone who had a similar passion to serve and empower women. Mary's heart has always been with women, and especially with those who are poor, marginalized, oppressed, and discounted. She is a proven community leader.

Second, Mary is fearless, especially regarding issues of injustice and oppression. She is also full of integrity and very much respected within the community and by her colleagues. While she can be outspoken on issues that are close to her heart, she is always diplomatic and open-minded.

Left, Feli and Mary Campbell at Labyrinth, 2018. Photo courtesy Chronicle Media, LLC.

Third, Mary has the skills to engage others and craft the right words on sensitive issues that touch the hearts of her audience. She has the stage appeal. I told her early on that it would be a disaster if I had to speak to a group of hundreds of people. So, we made a pact that she would be the spokesperson of Labyrinth while I would be her sidekick.

Fourth, Mary and I knew the partnership would be a learning experience for both of us. We vowed to talk, ask, listen, collaborate, and empower one another. There were many challenges we faced and were able to surmount, much too long to list. We shared frustrations, fears, tears, excitement, laughter, and victories as we worked together to make Labyrinth a reality for the women it would serve.

When I was tired and needed to take a break from our work, Mary led the program. When it was her turn to step out, I took over.

As we continued to develop Labyrinth's program, our bond deepened. I not only have found a collaborator of my dreams but a friend, a true friend.

During this time, as the non-profit struggled to gain momentum and find workspace and funding, I was approached by at least three individuals who encouraged us to help women who have criminal records. They wanted Labyrinth's client base to be comprised of women who were recently released from state prison or the local county jail, who were primarily reentering society on the west side of Bloomington.

Because of this interest, I was closely following the Bloomington Joy Care Center's successes and trials. The organization's sole purpose is helping male ex-offenders break the chains of recidivism and become productive members of society. We later learned a lot from former Judge Ron Dozier, president of the Joy Care Center's board, who was a tremendous asset and educated us on job training and mentoring programs.

I watched and I learned, but I was still hesitant to lead the charge to change Labyrinth's mission. Part of me was leery of helping those formerly incarcerated. My heart just wouldn't shift in that direction.

MCLP Fantastic Voyage Team 2013: Carlos T, Miranda, Anand Bhende, Feli, Chuck DiVerde, Mary, Ann Perry, Fernando Cornejo, and Tereva Parham.

9 LABYRINTH SHIFTS ITS FOCUS

While I was hesitant to alter our focus from helping homeless single women to those who were formerly incarcerated, our existing program continued to face increasing challenges. I decided that a shift was what we needed, that this was the impetus that would drive success. I chose to champion these women. Suddenly my goal was to convince the board of directors to do the same.

It was an uphill battle. We finally came together to shift our mission and changed our name from Labyrinth House to Labyrinth Outreach Services to Women in April 2009. We continued looking for a facility where we could house our clients and run our program. We were perpetually short on cash, but long on passion.

As we ran into obstacle after obstacle, I began to waver in my support. I decided to resign as board president in 2010. I felt ill-prepared to lead the organization in its new direction. I also had continued reservations about helping women who were formerly incarcerated. I had never even met someone who had served time, much less counseled them.

The board would not accept my resignation.

My whole life, I was told to stay away from criminals. Growing up in the Philippines, this was drilled into me. These were "bad" people who broke the law. They stole from others; they hurt people. I was also afraid and doubtful the community would support the program. We had four years' experience helping women without felony records and had not been met with much success. I was unsure how successful we could be helping women with records. Would the community back us up?

I thought the only way to confront my fear was to meet these women face-to-face. The next time we were told there were two women scheduled to be released to McLean County, I volunteered to interview them.

Another board member and I went to the Lincoln Correctional Center (now Logan Correctional Center) in Lincoln, Illinois. It was the first time I had stepped into a prison facility. It was awkward as we were asked to surrender everything we had: purse, wallet, cell phones, car keys, and coats. We were then led through a long, winding hallway that stopped in a small room next to an office. There were two chairs where my companion and I sat. A table divided us from a lone chair positioned in front of us.

As I listened to the first woman, Theresa*, share her story, I realized my fears were based on my bias. This woman could have been me. Different upbringings, but a series of bad circumstances and poor choices ultimately led her behind bars while I was on the outside looking in.

After that encounter, we educated ourselves as a board on helping this community of women. We contacted Sherrin Fitzer, Women and Family Services Administrator at Lincoln Correctional Center. She was a tremendous resource to us in navigating the prison system and the needs of women after they are released.

As I immersed myself in this work and became more involved with the women, I found out that my biases that these individuals are lazy, irresponsible, and dishonest were unjust. They have dreams and aspirations just like I do. They get hurt and angry, especially when an injustice was done to them. And they feel disappointed when they fail in their plans. These women have had all the odds stacked against them.

Many women in the program have drug convictions. The Labyrinth program does not accept women who have been convicted of sex crimes or murder charges for the safety of all the participants in the program. Many of the clients are younger women under the age of 40 and reflect the demographics of McLean County, which has an estimated population of 172,000. Some 83% of McLean County residents are Caucasian, 8% African American, 5.4% Asian, and 5% Latino, with a small percentage American Indian, Alaska Native, Native Hawaiian or Other Pacific Islander, or two or more races.[14]

At least 60% of Labyrinth clients were physically or sexually abused as a child or adolescent and/or were in violent abusive relationships. Fifty percent or more have mental illness because of the trauma they experienced from abuse, including major depression, bipolar disorder, or post-traumatic stress disorder (PTSD) that often goes undiagnosed and untreated. Many of them ended up using drugs or alcohol to block bad memories and flashbacks. Self-esteem issues, low cognitive abilities, or misdiagnosed or undiagnosed learning disabilities are other traits that clients may share. The combination of any of these issues with a criminal record may hold them back from successful job placements.

However, what we found through experience is that many of Labyrinth's clients could not hold a job because they lacked "soft job skills," which are a critical component for professional success. These include communication and interpersonal skills, such as dress code etiquette and work ethic. Many people learn these skills from their family, peers, and positive role models. Because of their dysfunctional family backgrounds and their unresolved traumas, many clients feel they cannot trust anyone. When they are told by their supervisors to redo a job, they react angrily and simply leave the job. So, many of the women cannot pass the 90-day probation period and sustain a job.

---

[14] *July 2018, https://www.census.gov/quickfacts/mcleancountyillinois*

Through Sharon Walker, Community Development Fiscal Officer for the City of Bloomington, we found a possible location for our nonprofit on Washington Street in west Bloomington. The house itself was demolished by the city due to its structural defects and the lot was empty and waiting. Architectural students from Professor Ryan Brown's class at Illinois State University created a design. Committees explored funding and a proposal to build a $300,000 Labyrinth House was presented to the Bloomington City Council in February 2012.

Denied. Again. That same month, the City of Bloomington approved $10,000 towards the project's counseling services but could not assist with housing. We just couldn't come up with enough money to fund the project.

It felt like we were hitting brick wall after brick wall.

In the fall of 2012, we hired a part-time counselor, Kate Nelson-Fagan, who worked with women released from Logan Correctional Center. Former CEO Rocky Ziegler of Mid Central Community Action donated office space to accommodate her. Even only working 10-20 hours per week, we began to make a difference by providing resources to formerly incarcerated women.

We were now providing services through our Labyrinth Outreach program, but we still did not have a home to call our own. A primary goal of the organization is to provide housing to our clients. Having a safe and stable environment for women who need it was necessary. We began to scour the community in earnest to find a building to house our program.

Research proved that for the women to be successful in rebuilding their lives in our program, they would need a stable living situation for at least 18 months. We investigated nearly 15 houses with the hopes that once we found one, we'd receive a grant or community funding. We nearly bought a house, but the offer fell through due to foreclosure complications. Every house we looked at raised our hopes, only to have them dashed. It was a lengthy process and we nearly gave up. We were running out of time though. We had received a $75,000 grant from the Community Development Block Grants (CDBG) in 2013 and we had to use it or lose it.

I did not let all the "noes" deter me. We continued to look for a property to rehab and renovate. We were exploring a few other options when a friend, Valerie Dumster, told Mary about two run-down homes on the west side of Bloomington with the right price tag. Mary Campbell had a vision for what the place could be from the minute we walked in. Her experience in renovating homes with her husband Hank was instrumental to our project. Hank acted as our consultant, giving us ideas on whether a house was salvageable and what the cost of renovations might be.

In the fall 2013, the property at 616 West Monroe and its adjacent multifamily property was purchased by John and Laurie Wollrab. John was a Labyrinth advocate, Bloomington businessman, and community leader. They bought the properties with the condition that Labyrinth would buy them back for the original price of $87,500 once renovations were complete. The properties were owned by Pontiac Bank, who was eager to sell. One of the properties was a two-story house with three bedrooms upstairs and a large living and dining room. It even had an unfinished basement. It had beautiful woodwork dating to 1918 and exuded personality. This would become our workspace.

As we did our walkthrough, I could hear Mary rattling off her plans of what to fix, how to fix it, and what to toss or keep. I was just listening and trying my best to imagine what she was saying. There was a lot of work to do, but we could manage it. Hank put in his own recommendations. Then we walked to the apartment next door. It was a four-unit apartment complex, with each unit made up of three bedrooms, a spacious living room, and kitchen/dining room. The fourplex had two units upstairs and two downstairs. Again, I heard Mary's ideas of how the units could be turned into the women's housing facility.

Now, the renovation work would begin, a process that would take nearly two years and many, many hands to shape.

My dream was becoming a reality.

10 SEEK, AND YOU SHALL FIND

Eight years after our house search began, we started renovations in 2013 on what would be Labyrinth's home. Mary knew all the contractors and people who would move our vision to realization as we renovated the two buildings; be it plumbers, electricians, or carpenters. She knew almost everyone in the community, ranging from a former student to an attorney to a community leader. And she had the history of the community at her fingertips. I learned about these beautiful people from the stories she shared with me, of their struggles and triumphs.

The renovation of the two condemned buildings began with assistance from high school students from YouthBuild of McLean County. YouthBuild's mission is to "build, develop, inspire and challenge educationally and economically disadvantaged students to make a difference." They certainly made a difference in our lives.

They came every day for several weeks to gut the two buildings. They tore out cabinets, toilets, carpets, and linoleum flooring, and hauled broken appliances and debris to the landfill. They worked very hard to make both buildings ready for repair and renovation.

We donated three beautiful antique bathtubs to the Historical Society to sell. Once the clearing out and cleaning was finished, Mary and I sat down and listed everything that needed to be repaired. We started with the exterior, then tackled each interior room. The first items that needed to be replaced were the exterior doors. Our first volunteer, Rich, hung up doors in the front and back of the house and each apartment unit. By the end of six weeks, he had hung 12 new beautiful doors.

Next, the windows had to be replaced with energy-efficient ones. Within two weeks, Window World installed lovely new windows in both buildings. A major overhaul of the electric systems followed. Upgraded bathrooms and kitchens were added to the first floor. The apartment building also required an electrical upgrade, given its age.

It was frustrating that we could not finish any work on the ceilings and walls because the electrician kept making hole after hole in them. We had to redo the walls several times. To give the house a new look, we had the floors sanded and re-stained. To make the doors in the house all uniform, we also re-varnished them one at a time. At the end of the day, I could not recognize my hands. They were reddish brown and sticky from the stain.

Seven days a week we had volunteers from all walks of life working on the rehabilitation project. Some of them were from area university fraternities and sororities, school groups, churches, civic organizations, local trade and labor unions, Habitat for Humanity, Recycling Furniture for Families, Fibers of Love, AMBUCS (AMerican BUsiness Clubs), Heartland Community College construction classes, small businesses, large companies, individuals, and families. Some came three to four times a week, others on weekends. We had grandparents and grandchildren, mothers and sons, brothers and sisters, husbands and wives, and teams, including a group of friends who came after their Saturday breakfast.

Labyrinth remodel in progress.

These generous individuals demolished drywall, scraped off paint and stain, cut and hung new drywall, painted ceilings and walls, pulled out staples from the floor, laid out tiles, and stained baseboards, doors, and stairs. More experienced volunteers oversaw carpentry.

I will never forget Lee, a volunteer who came once a week doing all types of jobs. One of his projects was tackling the concrete steps in the back of the house that had to be demolished so a deck and handicap ramp could be built. There were seven steps made of thick slabs of concrete. The whole thing was probably two or three feet wide and five feet tall. For several days, he worked on each step using a jackhammer that broke-up and crushed the cement. When he stopped for a break, he would show me his hands still shaking from the machine. He didn't stop until the last piece of the cement was pulverized. It was a job nobody wanted because the machine vibrates so strongly, and the vibrations were absorbed by his whole body. The cement clung to his hair, his clothes, his face, and even his eyelids. His whole body shimmered white with dust.

The back of Labyrinth and its former steps.

"Although the progress was slow, the miracles that unfolded during the renovation of the two buildings came in all forms."

The renovation work felt like a never-ending job. Each time we made progress with a room more repairs were identified. My to-do list seemed to be getting longer and longer, rather than shorter. I pitched in on anything I could do. Every day from 8:30 a.m. to 5 p.m., and sometimes later, I'd be at the job site, usually six days a week. I came home exhausted. My "break" was helping Mary write grants in the evenings and giving presentations in the community whenever she or I were asked.

Although the progress was slow, the miracles that unfolded during the renovation of the two buildings came in all forms. First were people who "found" Labyrinth to help renovate it. Each one had his/her own story to tell about why they volunteered. Slowly, I saw the house take shape, but I also witnessed the people who worked so hard blossom. Whether they volunteered for an hour, a day, or several weeks, they began to come together as a community; just like the ridges on the outer side of a labyrinth structure, each and every one was holding and supporting our women and the program. It became a sharing of lives moving in one direction with one goal: building a dwelling place for the women of Labyrinth.

By the summer of 2014, we were nearly halfway finished. The new Labyrinth Coordinator, Kristin Manzi, moved her office from the basement of Mid Central Community Action into the house. At this time, Labyrinth's mission grew to provide job coaching and counseling services, an addiction recovery support group, case management, and classes in life skills, along with limited housing for women. Women

Labyrinth House before (left) and after (right) renovations.

who are not housed within the Labyrinth Outreach walls can still receive outreach services.

The house was complete. The living room became a meeting room for the women's activities; a new office was built next to it; the handicap bathroom was done; the floors were stained and so were the stairs. Recycling Furniture for Families furnished the living room, the two bedrooms upstairs and the two kitchens. Fibers of Love volunteers sewed new covers for the donated couch and loveseat and quilts for each bed. The cabinets were installed, the appliances hooked up, and the windows were graced with new curtains. Kitchen utensils, tableware, pots and pans, tablecloths, and other kitchen stuff were organized by Deborah Hutchins, a devoted volunteer and board member. The house was looking great inside and out with the new siding coordinated by my nephew, Scott Barnett, who worked for James Hardie. Through his endorsement, James Hardie donated not just the siding, but everything we needed to replace the old siding: insulation, siding nails, boards, and glue. R.P. Lumber allowed us to store the materials in their facility until we found an installer.

Labyrinth apartments

The bulk of the remaining renovation was now focused on the four-unit apartment building. We prioritized which unit to repair first, dependent on the number of things that needed to be done. We started on the two upper units. Many of the walls and ceilings were intact so we just needed to repaint. The hardwood floors were restored by Mr. Sandless. While work was going on inside, groups of retirees and volunteers from Habitat for Humanity replaced the back siding of the apartment and re-built the roof of the front porch of the office/house next door. They were a fun group. Their only request was a snack of "monkey bread." I had to learn what it was and where to buy it. They reminded me of my maternal grandfather, who was also a carpenter. Fond memories of him building our house in the Philippines came flooding back to me. These men were just happy to help, and I loved listening to their jokes and banter.

The renovation story wouldn't be complete without talking about the silent, hard-working man who put up with me and Mary. Hank Campbell, Mary's husband, was our champion. He was our unofficial foreman, consultant, head carpenter, and handyman. He always moved our lofty ideas to a practical level. He told us when we were too absorbed about a small repair and losing sight of the total cost. He was wise and down to earth. We will be forever grateful for his guidance, energy, and dedication.

Another project was the building of a handicap-accessible ramp. Although none of our women at the time had a physical disability, building codes and ordinances mandated that we comply by providing a ramp. To have it in front of the house would ruin its beautiful facade, so it had to be built on the back of the house. To accomplish this, we had to do several things: 1) cut down the huge tree between the apartment and the office, 2) pulverize the concrete steps in the back, 3) create a curb on the sidewalk, 4) create a driveway between the two buildings, and 5) secure the two properties with a fence. AMBUCS was willing to build the ramp if there was a plan. A Heartland Community College construction class led by Professor Randy Jacobs designed the ramp and AMBUCS built it under the supervision of Alan Bedell. When the semester ended, the ramp was finished. It snaked out from the back door and into the backyard along the driveway. The students also added a bonus deck!

Many of our clients have suffered from one form of violence or another. They need to feel safe physically in the place they live so they can be at peace internally. The two properties' backyards used to be a shortcut for the neighbors to get to a nearby bus stop. However, drug dealers and criminals running away from police have also used our backyard as a hideout or quick escape. We knew we had to erect a fence to enclose the two buildings to give the women the feeling of safety they needed. However, we had already spent most of our budget. We knew we needed nearly $6,000 to buy a quality fence. We were fortunate that an anonymous donor stepped forward to finance the project, but were disheartened when just a week later, someone vandalized it by knocking down two panels and punching holes in them. We called the installer and they fixed it, but then it happened again the next week. We called the Bloomington police to patrol the area, which put a stop to it. Another safety feature we installed was a security system. It served a double purpose – to monitor arrivals and departures at night after the evening staff had left, and to deter unwanted intruders. For A Better Tomorrow, another local organization, donated money for cameras and volunteered to install them. In addition, the two outside electric bulbs in the corner lots were exchanged for bigger, brighter ones. With the backyard well-lit, surveillance cameras installed, and the fence erected, we believed the women would be safe.

For a final touch, Chris Kraft, a Master Gardener and a fellow Benedictine Oblate, along with the help of some Master Naturalists, landscaped the Labyrinth House and introduced gardening to our women. For most of them, it was their first time to plant and care for a living thing. One woman came every day after work to check on her plant. She said, "I never had this experience before. It feels good to care for something."

Once the apartment refurbishment was complete in October 2015, our first clients moved in. According to our guidelines, women are free to stay for up to two years while they reestablish their lives. At any given time, there have been 10-30 women who receive outreach services, such as assistance with child reunification, case management, job coaching and training, medical and psychiatric referrals, and addiction rehabilitation from Chestnut Health Systems. Labyrinth clients also participate in weekly meetings with staff to address relapse prevention, healthy relationships, self-care, and trauma recovery.

11 EVOLUTION

Labyrinth continued to evolve. With the house complete, it was time to turn over the reins. For the long-term viability of the program, we knew we had to partner with an agency with sustained leadership and economic stability. In 2016, we reached an agreement with YWCA McLean County to merge the Labyrinth program with the YWCA's Prevention and Empowerment Department. Currently, the YWCA staff are working on improving Labyrinth's two major programs – Mentoring and Micro Business. Once these programs are fully operational, they will be instrumental in lowering the recidivism rate of incarcerated women in our county.

From left, Feli Sebastian, Dontae Latson and Mary Campbell at the YWCA- Labyrinth Merging, July 1 2016.

Labyrinth's Mentoring Program

During our research and inspirational trip to the St. Louis Women in Transition Center, we were told that their recidivism rate rests in the single digits. When we asked how they achieved this, they noted the key is their mentorship program. All their clients are matched with a mentor who provides affirmation, support, and guidance. The mentors actively take these women under their wings as they live in the on-site housing program or receive services from the program. Their women meet with their mentors weekly to address and find resolutions to daily challenges they encounter at work or with family, continuing education, their addiction or relapse, and any other barriers these women encounter.

Following their model, a curriculum was developed for mentor training. When the Mentoring Program was first started in 2017, eight trained mentors were matched with eight mentees and they met regularly. Through experience and studies, we learned that weekly contact between the women and their counselor or program coordinator is not enough for them to manage all the demands put on them. These women need someone in their lives they can trust with their challenges and trials on an ongoing basis. They need a shoulder to cry on, an unbiased person who will understand their trials and still hold them accountable for their actions. These mentors are companions, confidants, and guides. Sometimes the mentor may have walked a similar path to her mentee. Oftentimes, they work together and both groups grow from the experience.

Currently, the staff continues to recruit and train mentors, as they are vital in helping the women rebuild their lives.

Labyrinth's Micro Business Program

Labyrinth has experimented with several types of micro businesses since its onset. We took our model from two other non-profit organizations – Thistle Farms of Nashville, Tennessee and Women's Bean Project of Denver, Colorado. These organizations both serve formerly incarcerated women. To boot, these organizations have had their micro businesses running for 25-plus years. They started from humble beginnings and grew to generate millions in revenue to fund their programs. Their shared philosophy is to have their clients work in a home-grown company to hone their skills. Some of them "graduate" from the company and gain employment in other local businesses, while others stay on at the company and fill important manufacturing and management positions. Not only do these women work at supporting themselves, they are also living role models for women entering the program.

An Illinois State University business class helped us brainstorm a micro business plan. Labyrinth wanted to produce safe, environmentally friendly, hypo-allergenic cleaning products. The class researched and found possible products Labyrinth could package, everything from laundry detergent, fabric softener, and soaps to other household cleaning products. The following semester, a business intern came up with a name for the business, "The Clean Slate Project." How clever to find the perfect name! It symbolizes our women's journeys as they rebuild their lives after serving their prison sentences – starting over with a clean slate.

Mary and I introduced the micro business to the community through invention fairs and entered contests to create awareness in the region. We also sought local and state grants to help in the funding of the business. We connected with the Service Corps of Retired Executives (SCORE), a national non-profit association dedicated to entrepreneur education and formation, and small businesses mentoring. The Illinois Small Business Development Center (SBDC), ISU entrepreneurship classes, and other agencies also gave us direction in marketing, business plans and proposals, and the endless list of things to consider when starting a business.

By the time Labyrinth partnered with YWCA, the program was ready for another update. For the second time, Multicultural Leadership Program (MCLP) sponsored Labyrinth. The MCLP team was very dedicated and committed to the project. They made significant recommendations for improvements, including marketing and product and logo development. At the end of nine months, MCLP announced that they would continue to work with the Labyrinth executive team to consider the legal aspects of setting up a for-profit business managed by a non-profit organization. After the executive team's visit and consultation with Thistle Farms in 2018, they decided to put a hold on the cleaning products project. With input from the women residents, other products, such as boutique crafts, were explored. Ultimately, the executive team chose to pursue a candle business.

The main idea in establishing a microbusiness that Labyrinth's clients can work within is to better the community while these women are bettering themselves. Clients can continue to develop their job skills and confidence before entering the permanent workforce. In 2019, YWCA Labyrinth was awarded $75,000 from the Google Impact Illinois Challenge. This money was used for hiring staff who directly manage the micro business, specifically the manufacturing, packaging, and sale of candle products. Like walking a labyrinth, setting up a micro business has had a lot of dead ends. There has been building and rebuilding; evaluating and re-evaluating every move and recommendation. Small progress has been achieved while more monumental decisions still need to be made. If we continue to keep our focus on the goal – the women and their families will benefit from the hard work. We cannot lose hope, nor can we forsake these women who depend on us. It will happen. We are convinced of this as our two model organizations have shown us. And we are determined to make it a reality, just like we did in our journey in establishing the organization and its facilities.

YWCA Labyrinth Outreach Support Continues

Labyrinth's relationship with YWCA began when its former CEO, Jane Chamberlain, endorsed the organization to the City of Bloomington Council in 2012 when Mary and I petitioned for a housing grant. She paved the way for that relationship to grow until Dontae Latson assumed his position as CEO in 2013. Several meetings with him and the YWCA Board ensued to identify and formulate the parameters for merging the two organizations. It took us three years to finalize the merger.

In the meantime, Labyrinth continued to grow and expand its program. It has worked to reduce the probability the women will return to prison by addressing their reentry needs through various services, including counseling, job coaching, and temporary housing. However, women must be ready and motivated to find success while owning their mistakes. They must be willing to navigate their reentry into the community, follow parole regulations, provide healthcare for themselves and their families, find a job and establish their identity, oftentimes without the support of former acquaintances who may have been negative influences in their lives. While some may stop using substances and never look back, others may relapse one or multiple times prior to stopping for good. The majority of the women we serve continue to stay in the process of recovery by not giving up. Other women may not struggle with substance abuse but will face the challenges of learning to build healthy relationships.

Vocational training and education are primary Labyrinth services. Finding a job is often a woman's number one goal when they are released from prison. They must find a job to sustain themselves and their children. Oftentimes having a job is a prerequisite to be reunited with their children. Labyrinth started its first vocational training in the spring of 2013. With the collaboration of the trades and labor unions, a curriculum was set up to give Labyrinth clients the opportunity to learn about basic carpentry, electrical, metal sheeting, roofing, and siding. Additional classes on flower arranging, soap-making, and crafts were also offered.

We collaborated with the local trades and union officers because these careers pay higher than minimum wage and do not discriminate against formerly incarcerated people. Women enrolled in the Trades Information/Education program met twice a week for 12 weeks, listening to experts in various fields and visiting plants and factories to gain hands-on experience.

Participants discovered that there is another world of opportunities for them on an untraditional path. They can earn a wage comparable to that of their male counterparts, sometimes even more. At the end of the program, participants graduated. Certificates were handed out to the women, who were adorned in a cap and gown. One of the women said through her tears, "This is awesome. This is the first time in my life that I finished something I started."

In the summer of 2014, the women were offered a Photography/Art Seminar called "A New Vision of Me." The group met once a week for eight weeks for a couple hours and learned about photography, painting using different mediums, sewing quilts, creating collages, and writing prose and poetry. The art, photography, quilts, paintings, poems and prose they produced were insightful and amazing!

Their weekly art group quickly became a support group. They began to talk and share their lives, their similar journeys and challenges, reasons they went to prison, and their hopes and aspirations as they rebuilt their lives. One of them poignantly shared, "I'm beginning to feel less ashamed of the mistakes I've made. I was stupid and stubborn. I feel there is hope for me." Another added, "I forgive my parents and myself."

In July 2016, Labyrinth merged with YWCA. Labyrinth gifted YWCA two mortgage-free, fully renovated buildings (the office and the four-unit apartment building), a full-time director, part-time staff for job coaching funded by the local United Way, and case managers/residential counselors funded by McLean County Health Department. YWCA continued, under the new leadership of CEO Liz German, these existing programs and strengthened Labyrinth's collaboration with other community resource partners.

According to the YWCA 2018 annual report,[15] the organization provided services to 112 formerly incarcerated women. This included

---

[15] *https://www.ywcamclean.org/who-we-are/annual-report*

assisting the eight women living in the on-site apartment building, as well as outreach clients. The women received 636 hours of group education and the organization's goals include: providing evidence-based reentry services to formerly incarcerated women, utilizing the Women's Needs/Risk Assessment (WRNA) to screen and identify individuals for treatment and reentry planning, and developing individual service plans for each participant.

In 2018, YWCA was awarded nearly $800,000 under the federal government's Second Chance Grant based on the above-cited report. The money supports funding for a full-time case manager and part-time residential counselors, economic specialists, and a mentor specialist. The grant is also being used to develop a system to collect data and track the recidivism rates of women in the program, as well as follow-up with those who have graduated from the program.

All the above is based on ongoing case management to ultimately reduce the recidivism rate which, according to a 2016 Illinois study, was 43% within three years and 17% within one year.[16] In 2018, Illinois reported that the housing cost to incarcerate an individual is $39,858 per year. The total economic impact of incarceration per year is $151,700, which accounts for lost wages, cost of housing, and associated indirect costs, such as reduced economic activity since former prisoners who recidivate no longer earn salaries, pay taxes, or otherwise contribute to their communities.[17]

Many of these women lost guardianship of their children, sometimes permanently. For those who have a chance at reconnecting with their children, who are oftentimes being cared for by extended family, this opportunity is the primary motivator for change. Two major universal goals of these women are to reestablish child custody and find a job. Occasionally these women are pregnant before being incarcerated. Some women place their baby for adoption while others leave their baby in care of family while they serve their sentences.

---

[16] *icjia.state.il.us*

[17] *https://www.prisonlegalnews.org/news/2019/feb/5/illinois-calculates-high-costs-recidivism/*

A lot of our clients' weaknesses include men. The need to be loved and belong is so strong, and oftentimes these women are victimized by those they love. When these women don't get the love they need from their family of origin, they turn to men. When they are rejected by the men in their lives, they find themselves in a bad place. It can be a vicious cycle.

If clients want reunification with their children – and most do – the requirements are many. Even if they did horrible things and were imprisoned and served their time, their heart is still the heart of a mother. They know a lot needs to be done to make up for whatever hurt they've caused their families.

Depending on the severity of their addiction or other problems, some women in the Labyrinth program could have already relinquished their parental rights. If they still have visitation rights, the Logan Correctional Center has established a "Mom and Me Camp" program, which is scheduled each July. Children who are 12 years old and younger and their caregivers can reconnect with their incarcerated loved one and enjoy a three-day visit. Half of the day, they visit their loved one, and the other half they attend East Bay Camp at Lake Bloomington, where they are free to enjoy camping and other outdoor activities. It also gives caregivers a short break from child-rearing.

Sherrin Fitzer leads this initiative and Labyrinth has supported it by donating money and volunteering in the camp activities. Labyrinth also has supported another program at Logan Correctional Center through a donation of parenting books used in parenting skills classes. The women take a course and read the books to better care for their children upon release. The more these women are exposed to positive changes and education in prison, the easier our job becomes at Labyrinth. These women hit the ground ready to change and are motivated to improve their lives.

However, not every client is a success story. Sometimes these women haven't come to a place of acceptance. They blame their parents, boyfriend, spouse, or society, among others. Failure to rehabilitate often includes drug or alcohol addiction, lack of job skills, low or under-education, poor social skills and mental habits, and a lack of money.

According to the 2018 Women's Whole Pie Report[18] produced in collaboration with the American Civil Liberty Unions Campaign for Smart Justice, 219,000 women are incarcerated in the U.S. There are 89,000 women in local jails and 99,000 in prisons. Federal prison comprised 16,000 inmates, immigration detention 7,000, and youth detention 7,300. According to the 2017 Report by World Prison Brief[19], the U.S. holds the highest female prison population rate at 65.7 per 100,000 of the national population.

Labyrinth has based its local services on successful models developed elsewhere. We've combined successful elements of programs in Denver, Nashville, and St. Louis. As our program evolves, we hope to better track our successes and significantly reduce the recidivism rates in Illinois, which are otherwise increasing. According to the Illinois Sentencing Policy Advisory Council,[20] over 40% of released inmates will return to prison in three years. The longer an offender goes without being re-arrested, the less likely they are to return to prison.

"These successful programs, they've been around for 20-plus years. They have that recidivism number down in the single digits," added Mary Campbell. That is where Labyrinth aspires its program to be.

Director of YWCA Labyrinth Kara Kirk added, "Through the Labyrinth program, many women have changed their lives for the better, but personal recovery and success looks different for each individual. Our goal is to walk with each woman on their journey to independence, assisting them with their personal goals and providing ongoing support."

Because these women feel safe and accepted at Labyrinth, they have made the following strides since 2015:

---

[18] *https://www.prisonpolicy.org/reports/pie2018women.html*
[19] *https://www.prisonpolicy.org/reports/pie2017women.html*
[20] *https://www.illinoispolicy.org/report-recidivism-to-cost-illinois-more-than-13b-over-next-5-years/*

- Approximately 40 women have moved into their own apartment.
- Three have opened her own business.
- Two participants have earned her GED.
- Several have returned to school to further their education, whether it be working towards their GED, college courses, or specific certifications.
- Two to three women find jobs monthly.
- Several have re-connected with their children and started regular visits.
- A couple of the women joined the Women's Justice Initiative Task Force in Chicago where their stories, experiences, and opinions about incarceration will help shape policy changes. The goal of the Task Force is to cut female incarceration by 50%.

Feli using the Figure Notes system.

Within the Labyrinth program every single day isn't filled with work, meetings, and improvement. Sometimes the women relax and take refuge in crafts, yoga, reading, and learning new hobbies. One of the newer initiatives is the Labyrinth band. Using a music program called Figure Notes, beginners can learn to play a song within an hour, no note-reading required. Each note is color- and shape-coded. Several members from the community and the Labyrinth Board donated instruments to the group.

It's important for these women to find success, even if that success is playing "Mary Had a Little Lamb." Some women have attention span issues and don't have the concentration to learn an instrument on top of all the other skills they are learning. However, this is a great way for them to have fun, be creative, and reduce their stress. What really strikes me is the joy in their eyes. Even if it's only for half an hour, to see that joy and happiness is a gift. It gives me hope that they'll connect that joy to other areas of their lives.

It's a miracle!

"It's a miracle!" We have heard this phrase many times. We have read it many times. We have wished it to happen, prayed for it to happen to us, to our loved ones, to others – whether the intention is for a cure of a terminal disease, an addiction, a broken relationship, or sustaining a hardship.

However, we fail to acknowledge that miracles happen every day in all forms and circumstances. Most of the ones we recognize are exterior or visual, such as being cured from cancer, being reconciled with someone, or recovering from an addiction. Others that are equally miraculous are often subtle and barely noticed because they occur within our innermost being.

Several former clients of Labyrinth reflect this transformation, and I believe everyone who walks through our doors and is committed to change can affect the same. Mandy* was a client who had experience painting houses. Upon her release, she tried to find a job that matched her skill set. However, no one would hire her. She decided to take a risk and start her own painting company, calling upon family and friends and a small nest egg of money she had saved to help her get established. Today, she employs a crew of painters and is

The women of Labyrinth enjoy "A New Vision of Me," a photography/art series.

successfully managing her own business. She even volunteered to paint our apartment building's interior. One of her finest moments, however, was when she volunteered to speak at the Summit of Hope Conference, a reentry program to help reduce the rate of recidivism. She addressed the women prisoners at Logan Correctional Center and shared her story. It was touching to see her glow with pride as she encouraged her peers that they, too, can transform their lives.

Another former prisoner named Lisa* also has a transformative story. Lisa, who had no addiction issues herself, was incarcerated for selling drugs. She said she went with the wrong crowd because she was "darn spoiled" – her words not mine. She wanted everything and anything without exerting effort for it. She was cocky and arrogant, characteristics that contributed to her time spent in prison. She said her prison sentence was a wake-up call for her. She owned up to her mistakes. It was a hard lesson to learn, but something she kept in the front of her mind to help her stay on course when she was released and looking to rebuild her life. She now owns a nail and hair salon business and helps other women achieve their goals by mentoring them and serving on the Women's Justice Initiative Task Force.

Mary* is yet another example of not only rehabilitation, but of redemption. Mary battled years of addiction and was convicted of forgery. Her addiction and prison sentence resulted in her losing custody of all of her children. They were placed in foster care. She herself was a ward of state as a child. Mary knew that the only way she could survive and regain custody was to pick up and repair her broken pieces and stay clean. She found faith, and slowly rebuilt herself until she regained custody of her children. She now helps other women navigate the court system as they go through the reunification process.

Looking back on the journey of Labyrinth, I observed the miracles that happened more subtly as well. Although the visual signs were there, the miracles of the heart that happened were more profound. I see miracles of the heart as a process of transformation. It was the transformation of hearts that brought together each and every one of the individuals who played important roles in making Labyrinth a reality. Each one has a miracle story to tell and retell. Each one has touched and was touched by everyone involved in the making of Labyrinth.

And the miracles continue to happen at 616 West Monroe today. Every individual who became part of Labyrinth's journey – from the volunteers, the staff, the women, and their families, has benefited as they continue on their journey. All because each one was willing to be open to the spirit and the movement that continues to unfold at Labyrinth. Each one was transformed in one way or another. And I speak from experience. Being part of the Labyrinth miracle made me more grateful for all the blessings that I used to take for granted. I have become appreciative of everything and accepting of things that come my way. I am by no means perfect. I continue to unfold, to walk the labyrinth of my life, to rediscover a better version of myself.

In December 2018, I was awarded the American Psychological Association (APA) Citizen Psychologist Presidential Citation for sustained community engagement and leadership for my role in creating Labyrinth. I was humbled by this honor and continue to support Labyrinth through my position on the YWCA Board.

It may be easy to dismiss someone due to their criminal history and unsavory aspects of their past. But they have paid for their mistakes; they have served their sentence. They need you and me to give them a second chance, even if only to change our preconceived ideas about them. I challenge you to shift your perspective, to reach out to one another in faith and love.

This banner shows the signatures of Labyrinth volunteers and donors. Banner compliments of Connie Mandula CM Promotions, Bloomington, 2014.

12 WHAT'S ON THE HORIZON

Now that Labyrinth is in good hands with YWCA McLean County and my involvement is limited to my position on the board of directors, I have been helping Mary Campbell develop a new organization to empower women to earn living wages and lessen the gender gap in the trades.

The new 501(c)(3) called Dreams Are Possible is housed at 1311 West Olive Street in Bloomington, a former grocery store with converted apartments on the second level. The lower half of the space has been converted into a job training site that works with existing job training programs at Mid Central Community Action, building-trades apprenticeships, job retraining efforts at Heartland Community College, Habitat for Humanity Women Build, and West Bloomington's Revitalization Project's Tool Library, among others. Home Depot donated over $10,000 towards the remodel, and several agencies, civic groups and individuals volunteered to landscape, paint and further enhance the property. A colorful mural was also painted on the building's exterior by many volunteers and the Youth Global Citizen group. The mural depicts women performing various trade jobs.

Logo created by Sherri McElroy.

Dreams Are Possible renovations.

The Dreams Are Possible mission is "to prepare women for economically sustainable employment by creating first class, skill-based workers; helping them transition from jobs to careers; and preparing them to expect and advocate for a living wage, benefits, and dignity in the workplace."

The program not only collaborates on training and education but is also working to provide mentors or coaches to support its participants.

"We really wanted to start a program for women of all ages who struggle, women who can't make that leap from the minimum wage-level job to sustainable employment or a career because they need further training and education," added Mary.

The program will be a bridge for women to move toward better, more livable employment. Training will help lessen the wage gap between economic classes of people and professions, reducing the 49-cent wage gap. This gap is even higher for women of color. Locally, 14.2% fall below the poverty line and 23,485 of 174,879 people living in McLean County fall into the poverty gap, earning minimum wage.[21]

The non-profit held its Open House in December 2019 and the first entry level class graduated in February 2020.

---

[21] *2014 Census, https://www.census.gov/quickfacts/mcleancountyillinois*

Dreams Are Possible was established to build a bridge and close a gap. Won't you help? More information is available at www.dreamsarepossible.org.

The mural was designed by retired Art teacher, Bonnie Bernardi, a long-time supporter of Labyrinth and Dreams Are Possible. The historic painted advertising above the mural was restored by Doug DeLong. From left, Feli and Mary in front of the mural at Dreams Are Possible by Mosaic Collective, LLC. Oct. 2019.

13 WITHOUT VOLUNTEERS, COLLABORATORS & DONORS, THERE WOULD BE NO LABYRINTH

Our volunteers come from all walks of life. Each person has his or her own story to share about why they support Labyrinth and helped build it. However, the common thread that led them to the doors of Labyrinth is compassion – compassion to help these women restore their lives, compassion to empower them, compassion to help them recapture their freedom and dignity.

From 2004 to 2008, Jeff Tinervin of First Site and Father Howard Bowlin of Christ the King Episcopalian Church were the driving force in finding a home for the Labyrinth House. It was through their contacts that we were able to explore many possibilities.

Despite our failed efforts to find a home for the women, Labyrinth House had a website: www.labyrinthhouse.org. It was created by my nephews from Canada; Telo Santos designed it and Marc de Castro financed its domain through his company Mardec Group Inc. Later, the MCLP Fantastic Voyage team updated our website to www.labyrinthoutreach.org.

The farthest volunteers traveled was from the Middle East and Amsterdam. The volunteers from the Middle East were Friends Forever participants who were training during the summer of 2014. There were twelve teens ages 14 to 17 who came from Israel and Palestine. They came to Bloomington to learn how to live peacefully within their own torn country, to learn a better way to relate to one another and become friends. The group came on a Saturday morning with their adult leaders and chaperones. They painted the kitchen and cabinets in the upper residential units. Being young and carefree, they ended their volunteer time painting one another. Their faces, hands, arms, hair were white, yellow, and green. They were laughing and giggling and chasing each other. No one was angry or offended. The playfulness and pure fun emanated from their hearts crossing cultures, religions, and social class. They were just happy human beings. Jews and Muslims became one community. I stood there watching them, watching the miracle unfolding right before my eyes!

The family from Amsterdam were friends of ours visiting in the spring of 2015. Our conversation turned to Labyrinth and their daughter Jocbeth was very insistent to see the facilities and help. One morning, we rose early, and we were able to squeeze in a couple hours of painting.

Another honorable mention is Sandy Bush, who stopped by the house a few months into our renovation project and asked for a tour. She had read about the project in the local paper. She asked a lot of questions and, at the end of the tour, asked what Labyrinth needed next. Mary and I said all the grant money from the Community Development Blocks Grant (CDBG) had been used for the major expenses and funding was still needed for the kitchen cabinets for the two buildings. Without hesitation, she pulled out her checkbook and wrote a $10,000 check to Labyrinth. We were astounded. Before leaving, she said to keep in touch if we needed anything else. I felt like the Master Plan was coming together and that our Divine Architect had long known our plans.

And, of course, many sincere thanks to the Labyrinth Board of Directors, especially the members who served from 2005-17. You have my deepest and sincere gratitude for your time, skills, talents, and support. Without your belief in our mission, we would not have brought Labyrinth into fruition. I appreciate and value all of you.

Peter*: During the summer of 2014, Peter came knocking on Labyrinth's door. He knew Hank and had previously worked for him. He was tall, strong, and good-looking. He was also quick to learn any type of work once it was demonstrated. He came every day and worked as Hank's assistant, learning to do more complicated carpentry jobs as the work continued. We became friends and soon enough, I became his "assistant." Together we laid out hardwood floor and tiles in the apartments and stained the stairs of the house. As the days went by, he took on more important jobs and both of us were put in charge when Mary and Hank were out of town. We became good teammates. We worked quickly and moved from one project to the next. He was instrumental in helping us meet our Open House deadline of December 2014.

As our days on the job together grew, so did our friendship. But he slowly began to change. He missed work. He looked dazed when he was there and was always telling sad, sobbing stories. Then he abruptly disappeared. Unfortunately, he had relapsed into his former lifestyle. My heart went out to him because he had been doing so well, but sadly his story is not uncommon. It is a life-long battle for addicts to conquer their demons.

IGate is a group of State Farm contract workers from India. This group of men and women came the very first day we had a volunteer day. The men worked on clearing the backyard, hauling heavy debris to the curb, and carrying furniture up and down from the upper units. They helped hang ceiling fans and moved appliances. The women cleaned walls, painted, and organized the endless clutter. This group volunteered until the house and the apartments were finished. Their support continues to pour in. Their children got involved with

SEWA International, a Hindu faith-based humanitarian, nonprofit organization that aids local communities. They have collected and donated nonperishable food for the women every year. They also participated in our fundraising efforts through garage sales and "Chairs 4 Change," a fund raiser where old chairs are colorfully repainted and auctioned.

Julie Roth & Sabrina Burkiewicz: Julie and Sabrina are young, energetic, passionate officers of Home Sweet Home Ministries, a local homelessness resource center. They are a dynamic team who developed and enriched their organization's programs. At the very start of Labyrinth, they were my guiding lights. They taught me everything I needed to know about establishing a non-profit organization. They taught me the technicalities, but they also showed me the perseverance and stamina I needed to overcome the many obstacles we faced as an organization. They inspired me. They taught me everything they knew and shared generously. They taught me how to stay on top of things – from how to stay focused on the Labyrinth's mission, to how to develop a vision statement, to how to connect with our target population. They were instrumental in helping me establish and maintain relationships with supporters. In 2007, they helped our board evaluate Labyrinth: its mission, goals, and future steps. This helped the board outline the blueprint of the organization and prepare its next steps. What touched me about this duo were their big hearts. I felt that they were my companions in the mission. They were always there to cheer me up or to rally with me when things were not going as planned. Julie and Sabrina were my first mentors in my non-profit endeavor.

Kristin Manzi, MSW: Kristin was Labyrinth's second-hired staff member but was already involved with the program a year before she was hired in March 2013. She came to us through a project for her macro social work class at Illinois State. Her group researched similar programs and made recommendations on improving ours.

"Hearing about Labyrinth was a new concept for me. I immediately felt that this was something I wanted to be a part of and use my trauma counseling to better these women's lives," Kristin added.

She came onboard after our part-time counselor resigned.

"I felt like anything could happen, but most likely we were going to change the world," Kristen said of joining the organization.

She started at 10 hours per week and gradually moved to 20 hours and then to full-time status as the program continued to ramp up. She initiated programs and counseled the women, established the reentry program, developed the interns' responsibilities, and acted as their supervisor. She also developed the mentoring program, ran support groups in the county jail, was an advocate for our clients, and attended community meetings and fairs to raise funds and spread the mission of the organization. She was Labyrinth's ambassador to the community. She met the women in Logan Correctional Center and interviewed them before they were released. And on top of these momentous tasks, she was also researching grants and other similar programs to collaborate with. In the four years she was with Labyrinth, she created the program and got it going. She was a superwoman, indeed!

"Although I felt like there were 12 steps still needed for every one we accomplished, we made great strides. In my time at Labyrinth I learned a lot about the clients and about myself," Kristin added. "I learned that saying 'no' and having boundaries as a counselor is not being mean. That when you tell someone you have been enabling them by giving them rides whenever they are running late, they will rise to the occasion and get to the bus on time. That some of the best conversations about a relapse come after saying, 'I don't think all of that is true' before the painful details come out. I am still growing, and I was gullible when I started working at Labyrinth. I did not try to fake the fact that I am a big dork from the suburbs of Chicago. I may not have necessarily had street cred, but I really cared about the women of Labyrinth. I also learned and grew from my colleagues who have personal experience in recovery and the legal system. They lent me their strength."

What made Kristin dear to the women she worked with was her innate ability to feel their pain and struggle. I have seen her cry with them, laugh with them and treat them with respect and dignity. She knew deeply in her heart the darkness these women lived through. To her, they were her sisters.

"I remember every person we helped. Every woman who graduated to their own apartment, got their kids back, got their first 'real' job, earned their GED, went back to school. One person even told me she bought a house! Even seemingly small victories, like getting off parole early because she earned the trust of parole officers, made me proud. But I also remember every person who gave up their apartment because they were convinced to move back with an abusive partner; every person who had to move out of Labyrinth because they were still using drugs. And I run into them and they're still using. They're still hurting. Some of them have had new charges filed or have returned to prison despite receiving services. Some discontinued services with us and walked away and we lost them back to the system. I try not to dwell on these, but I remember them, too," she noted.

Drake Zimmerman: Have you ever encountered a person who just exudes joy and generosity, in addition to being super intelligent and knowledgeable about almost anything, and remains humble? I certainly have. Drake Zimmerman embodies these characteristics. I was floored with his knowledge about our community, local and global profit and non-profit organizations, investments, and money, not to mention his ideas and working solutions to almost any problem in the world. Drake has been an important member of Alliance for Malaria Prevention in eradicating malaria in developing countries. He also has been a volunteer with Habitat for Humanity of McLean County for many years. He is someone who keeps giving his time, talents, and money to causes that improve people's lives and will advance humanity towards peace and justice.

When Drake learned that Labyrinth needed money to buy back its two properties on West Monroe from John and Laurie Wollrab, he did not hesitate to mobilize his resources to help launch a capital campaign. Through his guidance and direction, the board was able to raise more than $150,000 in less than a year. With that money, Labyrinth repaid the Wollrabs the $87,500 it owed for the properties and became the legal owners of the two buildings. The campaign was so successful that we had extra funds to install a fence to enclose the properties.

Ever since that time, Drake has become our guru on money matters and Labyrinth's loyal friend and supporter.

Interns – we couldn't have operated without them

2012 brought our first batch of student interns. They represented Illinois State University's Social Work department and Criminal and Justice departments. Daniel Anderson and Darci Thompson worked closely with our women specifically on vocational training. They prepared the syllabus, assisted in the discussion, gave the women rides, took the women on field trips and work site reviews, and provided the women extra resources on subjects that piqued their interests. Meanwhile, they also recorded data about the women who registered for the vocation training and measured changes in their self-esteem, attitudes toward work and authorities, social skills, and more. It was through their observations that we discovered our women lacked "soft job skills."

The women were also surprised to see a young man interested in their well-being without looking for "reward." One of them said, "I can't believe Daniel cares truly for me. It is the first time a man regarded me this way without using my body."

As the semesters rolled on, we received a steady supply of interns from Illinois State University and Illinois Wesleyan University. One of the interns was a former prisoner. She was a young woman who was just released and returned to finish her college degree. She said she had been naïve and made a grave mistake. While studying for her degree, she set up her own small catering company. The Labyrinth women could not believe she was at one time like them. Her presence gave the women hope that they, too, could be successful and happy, and free of their past.

Due to the vast amount of work that is needed to keep the programs going, some of the interns did behind-the-scenes jobs. While they were present and supported the women in their daily needs, such as providing transportation, others tackled "boring" paperwork and desk job tasks. One of those who was a data-driven intern was Kayla Gropp. She revised the board's policies and responsibilities, updated the donors list, and created all kinds of forms for the clients and the volunteers. What I so admired about her was she always did a job with a smile.

Additional Collaborators and Donors

Multicultural Leadership Program (MCLP); State Farm; United Way; Illinois State University construction classes; Harvest Family Worship Centre; McLean County Center for Human Services; Illinois Prairie Community Foundation; Illinois State University Communication Classes; McLean County Health Department; Project Oz and McLean County Sportsmen's Association were some of the initial supporters, collaborators and donors of Labyrinth.

Multicultural Leadership Program (MCLP): We were operating as Labyrinth Outreach Services to Women when we heard of MCLP. Someone suggested we apply for their services to help Labyrinth get more organized. At this point, our brochures were homemade, computer-generated, black and white trifolds and we had a website that needed upgrading as we had changed our mission statement to include formerly incarcerated women.

We were very much in need of help with big marketing tasks – creating a logo, updating our brochures and website, and establishing contacts with key community leaders, as well as small tasks like creating business cards and stationery.

Mary and I finished the MCLP grant application shortly before the midnight deadline. After a few months' wait, Labyrinth was named one of the five non-profit organizations the team leaders would assist. The team called themselves "Fantastic Voyage" and was comprised of five volunteers from various local companies who would donate nine months of mentorship as servant-leaders.

Before the first meeting with the team, I knew Mary was going to be out of town and I would have to represent Labyrinth. I prepared myself like I have never done before. I wanted to make a fantastic first impression on behalf of Labyrinth. I felt if I made an impact on them, they would connect better with the plight of our clients. My hope was that they would not only use their creative skills, but also empathize with the women of Labyrinth.

From that first meeting with Fantastic Voyage, Mary, the board, and I met regularly with the team as they progressed in their work. They developed a beautiful logo and we created a brand. They expanded our connections in the community with influential persons who were receptive to our cause. They introduced us to State Farm and its philanthropy program, connected us with the media – radio and television, and created videos for us to help with our presentations. They also updated our website. They found supporters who donated Labyrinth banners that we display at our presentations. It was a total makeover!

State Farm: State Farm was one of the larger companies who supported us. The members of the MCLP Fantastic Voyage helped connect us with State Farm's leadership in community development. Jerome Maddox was instantly receptive to our mission and provided the organization $25,000 to cover our vocational training. He also provided Mary and I invaluable leadership advice and recommendations on a plethora of issues. We christened him "Godfather of Labyrinth" for his steadfast continued support and friendship.

United Way of McLean County: In Labyrinth's early days, I sought out the CEO of United Way when I heard that there was potential that they could fund some of our program's initiatives. He listened to what I had to say and although he declined my request at the time, he was cordial and respectful. The agency just wasn't funding any new programming. I was discouraged, although by then I was used to being rejected.

However, a few years later when Labyrinth was operating as an outreach to the community's formerly incarcerated women, United Way sought us out, namely because our population served was the only one not represented by their agency. The collaboration began in 2016, and their non-profit funded the salary of our job coach for a three-year cycle! Lesson learned: patience. An initial "no" can become a "yes" if we wait long enough. Again, it was a lesson of trust in the Divine Plan.

Harvest Family Worship Centre: This is the first church that directly took care of our women. Dale and Tammy Miller, the husband and wife pastoral team, were very generous and receptive to our women's needs. I was so humbled when, after attending their services and concluding our Labyrinth presentation, we were presented with a $1,000 check. The members of this church generously gave from what little they had to help our women. They also welcomed our women to their Christmas service and dinner, again abundantly sharing.

First Labyrinth garage sale fundraiser. Left, Derek, sister Aline, nephew Michael, niece Deanna, and Feli.

Harvest Family Worship Centre also hosted our first garage sale fundraisers. The church members set up tables and donated things to sell. The first year we held it, it rained on the first day. I remember frantically covering stuff with tarps and hauling some of it inside the church. While we raised some money, our goal was to raise awareness about Labyrinth in the neighborhood. Many of the shoppers were our future neighbors and they appreciated helping in their own small way. A few of them even whispered in passing that they know either a family member or a friend who could benefit from the program.

This community continued to give back by hosting our Labyrinth board meetings in their church basement. Tammy later accepted our invitation to serve on the board.

McLean County Center for Human Services: Because more than 60%[22] of the women Labyrinth serves have been victims of trauma or abuse, they often suffer from anxiety, depression, post-traumatic stress disorder, bipolar disorder, and other mental illnesses. Some are fortunate to undergo counseling and/or receive medication during incarceration, but many of them do not have this opportunity. If their condition is severe, they get attended to while serving their sentence. However, many fall through the system and fail to get the psychological or psychiatric treatment they need. Others experience symptoms for years before receiving treatment.

If the women were on medication while incarcerated, when they are released, they are given a month's supply of medication. Without their medication, they are at risk of becoming vulnerable and fragile. Those first few weeks after being released are stressful as each woman adapts to her new environment and how best to comply with her post-release requirement list, as well as finding a job, reconnecting with their children, and finding a place to live. If these women can't find services to extend their prescription, they often resort to self-medication with alcohol and drugs.

Mary and I both knew that this would be a huge obstacle for our Labyrinth clients to overcome. We had to find a way for these clients to continue their prescriptions for a few months' time as they applied and were processed through the state's health care system. In order to

---

[22] *Based on Labyrinth internal data: 2013-15.*

apply for medical assistance, one needs to meet many requirements. One of those is obtaining a state ID. If a client had a driver's license before they were incarcerated, they need to apply for a new one or apply for a state ID card. In turn, those IDs are needed to apply for the Supplemental Nutrition Assistance Program (SNAP), employment, and medical assistance.

It was fortunate that Illinois Prairie Community Foundation opened applications for health grants around the time we needed them. Mary and I quickly applied and by the grace of God, Labyrinth was granted $5,000 for our clients to continue their medication needs until they were enrolled in state health plans. We knew the money would not last long, so we approached Tom Barr, CEO of the McLean County Center for Human Services, to partner with us. He agreed that their in-house psychiatrist would handle psychiatric assessments and medication management on a sliding-scale basis. The Labyrinth coordinator works closely with clients and the psychiatrist once she knows their needs for psychiatric services.

Illinois Prairie Community Foundation: Illinois Prairie Community Foundation was the first foundation that took us under their wing. They readily funded our projects that addressed the needs of the women of Labyrinth. They awarded us money for stop-gap medication funding and psychiatric assessments; they granted us money towards the vocational training of the women; and they supported Labyrinth's culture and photography project.

It was heart-warming to see Illinois Prairie Community Foundation believe in and support our mission. They understood that helping these women not only meant helping everyone in the program, but also their children and their families. Their support is for the betterment and overall health of the community.

McLean County Health Department: A few months before we completed our house renovations, we realized we needed to hire evening residential staff to stay on-site. One of the important recommendations the Center for Women in Transition in St. Louis made was to start with round-the-clock supervision.

However, we were strapped for money. Our program coordinator had just been promoted to full-time status and most of our money was paying off renovations and current staffing. The director of the Health Department, Laura Beavers, then directed us towards a grant that could help us fund the evening staff.

We applied for the grant, and while doing so, United Way of McLean County also announced a grant for a job coach. It was perfect timing! The women of Labyrinth needed both night supervision and a job coach. We received both grants and, in the fall of 2015, our first residents moved in. Soon our units were full, and we hired three part-time, dedicated night staff and a new part-time job coach.

Project Oz and the McLean County Sportsmen's Association: As we tore out the floors and ripped up the old carpets and linoleum, I knew we didn't have the money to replace them, but I also knew we'd find a way. Our nest egg of $75,000 was nearly spent on major construction materials. I prayed for a solution.

Sometime later, I received a call from a representative from the Sportsmen's Association. Their organization receives donations of discontinued items from Home Depot and then the club reaches out to local charities to donate and install the items.

They had a huge amount of construction materials to donate. I felt like we had won the lottery! Shortly after their initial call, the group of mostly retired men came armed with carpets, hardwood floors, doorknobs, faucets, bathroom mirrors, lamps, and more. I had to excuse myself to mop up my face of tears after witnessing all the generosity.

I felt this quiet peace inside me, a peace that reassured me that, "We are covered." We were provided for just like my mom would say when money was tight. I just had to learn to trust.

Do you know the line, "God will never be outdone in generosity."? Well, He proved it to me again. Just as we were getting this avalanche of construction materials from the Sportsmen's Association, Peter Rankaitis of Project Oz contacted us and said that his organization had a lot of unused construction materials that we could choose from.

I was dumbfounded when Mary, Hank, and I stood in Mid Central Community Action's 12,000 square foot basement surveying an assortment of tiles of all sizes and colors, doors, rolls of carpets, windows, and more. I felt like a kid in a candy store. More than anything, I felt a surge of gratefulness – gratefulness for their generosity and for God's provisions.

ISU Construction Class and Bloomington City Council:
During Labyrinth's Washington Street housing venture, we were connected with Professor Ryan Brown's architectural class. His class made Labyrinth their project. Bloomington's City Council required us to present a house plan for the lot on Washington, on which they would base their decision to fund us. The students produced a professional-grade house plan, complete with landscaping and estimated costs. It was these master plans which were presented to the Council. Although the plan was voted down due to cost, one of the Council members suggested that we look for existing houses that could be renovated for less and come back to the Council. They also suggested that we explore other existing shelters in the community. That suggestion led Mary and I to look for houses in the West Bloomington area, since most of the women moved back there after incarceration.

To strengthen the west side's support, we met with Home Association board members Rick and Susan Heiser several times. They understood us and the needs of these women. They also endorsed us during the two Council meetings in 2012 and 2013, where we discussed city support of Labyrinth and its mission. The Heisers supported these women like they were their own family members.

ISU Communication Students: To increase Labyrinth's online profile and visibility, we needed to produce videos. Mary's connection with Illinois State University allowed us to partner with communication students who produced a series of videos.

The first video was about the organization – its mission, goals, and vision. Two of our former clients volunteered to share a brief synopsis of their lives and what they hoped to achieve through Labyrinth's services.

The next video was longer and profiled a couple of board members, a local officer in the criminal justice system, and a former prisoner. The video highlighted the statistics of incarcerated women, reasons for incarceration, and needs after incarceration, including the programs Labyrinth offers.

The final video showcased the renovation of the two condemned properties that housed Labyrinth clients, as well as the office and meeting space the program utilized. All the videos were professionally done by this enthusiastic group of ISU students. They recorded the renovation and interviewed volunteers, board members, staff, donors, and Bloomington officials. These videos helped relay Labyrinth's mission and highlight the women served, which resulted in a fresh slew of support.

A compilation of videos on "Labyrinth Outreach Services" can be viewed on YouTube:
1. An overview, https://bit.ly/LabyrinthOutreach
2. Mary Campbell's TEDxNormal talk "Helping the Formerly Incarcerated Be Successful" at https://bit.ly/MaryCampbellTedxTalk
3. Feli Sebastian's story "Beloved" which was delivered at the event "That's What She Said" on September 27, 2019 and benefitted Labyrinth, https://bit.ly/FeliSebastianThatsWhatSheSaid

---

I'm sorry if I missed acknowledging anyone's contributions. Each and every donor and supporter of Labyrinth holds a special place in my heart, and I am forever grateful for the outpouring of support the organization has received. Love, Feli

Locations of local Labyrinth structures:
- Community Cancer Center, 407 E. Vernon Ave., Normal, IL
- Wesley United Methodist Church, 502 E. Front St., Bloomington, IL

Thank you for supporting Labyrinth Outreach Services by purchasing this book. A portion of the proceeds will support the program that is managed by YWCA McLean County, Illinois.

To make additional contributions, please see their website: www.ywcamclean.org/what-we-do/prevention-and-empowerment-services/labyrinth

That's What She Said Project, 2019, Bloomington, IL. Feli is second from the left. Reprinted with permission, That's What She Said Project.

ABOUT THE AUTHOR

Feli Sebastian is a retired licensed clinical psychologist and founder of Labyrinth Outreach Services to Women, a nonprofit organization that provides comprehensive aid to formerly incarcerated women when they return to their community. The organization merged with the YWCA McLean County (Illinois) on July 1, 2016.

She is on the YWCA Board of Directors. Sebastian is co-developer of start-up Dreams Are Possible, a non-profit venture started by friend and former Labyrinth Board Member Mary Campbell, which strives to help women find sustainable employment by providing them with free training and materials to learn trade jobs.

Sebastian is also on the board of Recycling Furniture for Families and For A Better Tomorrow. She was awarded the 2018 APA (American Psychological Association) Citizen Psychologist Award in 2018 for her sustained community engagement and leadership in working with underserved women and minority populations of McLean County. In 2014 she was presented the United Way Phil Covey Award.

Sebastian earned a BA in History at College of the Holy Spirit (Philippines), a BA in Religious Studies at Lourdes University (Ohio), a Master's in Guidance and Counseling at Ateneo de Manila (Philippines), and a Ph.D. in Counseling at The University of Toledo (Ohio).

She is an Oblate of St. Mary Monastery, Rock Island, Illinois.

"Broken & Beloved" is Sebastian's first book.